Justice and Christian Ethics is a study in the meaning and foundations of justice in modern society. Written from a theological perspective, its focus is upon the interaction of religion and law in their common pursuit of justice. Consideration is given, first, to the historical roots of justice in the classical tradition of virtue (Aristotle and Aquinas) and in the biblical ideas of covenant and the righteousness of God. Subsequent chapters trace the relationships between justice, law, and virtue in Puritanism, in Locke, and in the founding documents of the American Republic in the late eighteenth century. In his concluding section, the author develops a covenantal interpretation of justice which includes both law and virtue, both human rights and the common good. Special attention is given to the pluralistic character of modern political societies; to criteria of distributive justice; and to religious resources for the renewal and transformation of justice.

JUSTICE AND CHRISTIAN ETHICS

NEW STUDIES IN CHRISTIAN ETHICS

JUSTICE AND CHRISTIAN ETHICS

E. CLINTON GARDNER

Professor Emeritus of Christian Ethics,
Emory University, Atlanta

CAMBRIDGE
UNIVERSITY PRESS

Published by the Press Syndicate of the University of Cambridge
The Pitt Building, Trumpington Street, Cambridge CB2 1RP
40 West 20th Street, New York, NY 10011–4211, USA
10 Stamford Road, Oakleigh, Melbourne 3166, Australia

© Cambridge University Press 1995

First published 1995

Printed in Great Britain at the University Press, Cambridge

A catalogue record for this book is available from the British Library

Library of Congress cataloguing in publication data
Gardner, E. Clinton (Edward Clinton), 1920–

Justice and Christian ethics / E. Clinton Gardner.
p.   cm. – (New studies in Christian ethics)
Includes bibliographical references and index.
ISBN 0 521 49639 x
1. Christian ethics. 2. Justice. I. Title. II. Series.
BJ1275.G35   1995
241'.622–dc20   95–42267 CIP

ISBN 0 521 49639 x hardback

To Ruth
Beloved partner in marriage

Contents

General editor's preface

This book is the seventh in the series New Studies in Christian Ethics. As I had hoped, a distinctive shape is beginning to emerge in the series. Not only are contributors well-versed in one of the humanities, science or social science disciplines, they are also prepared to challenge some of the secularist assumptions that often underpin them in the modern university.

Kieran Cronin's *Rights and Christian Ethics*, the first book in the series, saw considerable areas of overlap between Christians and secularists in the debate about "rights." However he concluded that Christians (and indeed many others with religious faith) do have deeper "justifying reasons for acting morally" than secularists, precisely because moral behavior for Christians is a part of their relationship to God.

James Mackey's *Power and Christian Ethics* also offered a theological challenge to much secular thought. He argued that, in a world that frequently equates power with force, religious communities (despite their many failures) can have real significance. At best such communities offer a "radical and encompassing sense of life as grace" which "enlightens and empowers people to imagine and create an ever better life, and also to overcome the forces of destruction which one could otherwise only join and increase, but never beat."

Ian Markham's *Plurality and Christian Ethics* also offered a distinctive theological challenge. In arguing for a position of what he terms "constructive plurality," he maintained that secularism as a basis for rational dialogue in the modern world is surprisingly weak. In contrast, he argued that theism offers "a more coherent description of life than any alternative world perspective." He was in the end convinced by those who argue that it is theism which "makes sense of the objectivity of value and the intelligibility of the universe."

Of course others have made similar claims in the debate that is currently raging between modernists and postmodernists. However none of the writers in this series relies upon hyperbole or engages in dramatic end-of-the-Enlightenment discourse. Ian Markham was quite critical of such discourse, reminding his readers of some of the positive features of the Enlightenment as well as its inherent weaknesses. Rather, the dominant discourse in this series is that of a sustained dialogue with secular disciplines, albeit a critical and non-subservient dialogue.

Jean Porter's *Moral Action and Christian Ethics* offered another significant theological challenge to much secular moral philosophy. She was finally unconvinced by what she regards as the false security of many moral theories "with their promise of certainties that we cannot attain." Instead, she returned to Aquinas and sought to re-interpret his understanding of the moral act as a product of inter-dependent moral virtues. For her the moral life consists of a subtle interplay between human dignity grounded in restraint and forthrightness, kindliness and decency built up out of caring, and fairness and responsibility forming a basis for justice.

A study of the general theme of justice follows naturally from Jean Porter's book. It is also clearly of central importance both to Christian ethics and to moral thought today. For all of these reasons Clinton Gardner's *Justice and Christian Ethics* is particularly welcome in the series.

In the initial chapter of this book Professor Gardner makes a very imaginative use of Berman and sets out the challenge offered by a theistic understanding of justice. The second chapter relates usefully to the MacIntyre/Hauerwas debate – a debate which is a central one to the arguments of several of the contributions to the series. And the final chapter presents the case for taking seriously covenantal understandings of justice – understandings which Clinton Gardner shows have long been derived from biblical material, especially in America.

This is a very welcome and thorough study.

ROBIN GILL

Acknowledgments

This work is a study in the meaning of justice in Christian ethics. In this respect it represents a continuation of many years of reflection upon the nature and foundations of justice in theological ethics.

More specifically, however, the focus of the present project is upon the relationship of justice to law and virtue. How is justice understood as obedience to law related to justice understood as the practice of virtue? How does one move from abstract notions of law to the application of the law to particular cases? Conversely, if justice is conceived as the praxis of virtue, is law also necessary, as Aristotle suggests, to prevent just persons from committing unjust acts? My own reflection on such questions has been stimulated in recent years through participation in a number of interdisciplinary projects at Emory University involving faculty and students in the various professional schools, particularly law, medicine, and theology. In this regard, I want to express my profound gratitude to James T. Laney, formerly Dean of the School of Theology and subsequently President of Emory University, for his constant support of such projects. Special thanks are also due to Frank S. Alexander, Harold J. Berman, Jonas Robitscher, and John Witte, Jr., of the School of Law; and to Albert Brann, W. Newton Long, Theodore Hersh, and John H. Stone, of the School of Medicine. Each of these colleagues has enriched my own understanding of justice both in relation to their respective professions and in relation to public policy.

While it is impossible to mention the names of all who have contributed in significant ways to the development of the following essay, I am deeply grateful to Dean Jim L. Waits for his support in arranging a sabbatical leave (1986–87) in which to pursue research on Puritanism and John Locke. Special thanks are also due James M. Gustafson for his encouragement and critical suggestions at an early stage in the conceptualization of the project; to E. Brooks Holifield for his careful appraisal of recent Puritan scholarship; and to David Little for his interpretation of Puritan political thought and the modern human rights movement. I am also indebted to the staffs of Pitts Theology Library and the Robert W. Woodruff Library at Emory University and the Cambridge University Library for their generous assistance in making needed research materials available.

Portions of the materials included in chapters 2, 4, and 5 appeared previously in the following articles in *The Journal of Law and Religion*: "Justice, Virtue, and Law," *JLR*, vol. 2 (1984), no. 2; "Justice in the Puritan Covenantal Tradition," *JLR*, vol. 6 (1988, no. 1; and "John Locke: Justice and the Social Compact," *JLR*, vol. 9 (1992), no. 2. "Justice in the Puritan Covenantal Tradition" was published simultaneously in *The Annual of the Society of Christian Ethics* (1988). Permission to use these materials is gratefully acknowledged.

The Society of Christian Ethics has greatly enriched and broadened my understanding of justice, both as theory and as praxis, through the provision of an increasingly inclusive (religious, racial, and feminist) community of scholars and activists in the field.

In closing, I want to express my deep gratitude to Alex Wright, Religious Studies Editor, Cambridge University Press, for his constant support, his patience amid unforeseen delay in the completion of the manuscript, and his guidance and direction in bringing the latter to publication. I am also greatly indebted to Robin Gill, general editor of New Studies in Christian Ethics, for the inclusion of this book in that series. Special thanks are also due to Deborah McLauchlan and other members of the editorial staff for their assistance in preparing the final copy for publication.

CHAPTER I

Introduction

THE RELATIONS OF LAW AND RELIGION

Justice is the fundamental moral requirement of human life in community. Historically in Western culture, it has been a central concern both of law and of religion. Reflection on justice is a perennial theme not only in the classical political thought of Greece and Rome but also in the biblical understanding of the righteousness and sovereignty of God. Although justice has both a legal and a transcendent dimension in each of these traditions, its transcendent character achieves its fullest expression in the ethical monotheism of the Hebrew prophets of the sixth to the eighth centuries BC. While acknowledging that all three of these traditions have made major and distinctive contributions to the development of modern law, Harold Berman argues persuasively that the Western legal tradition as a whole rests upon the underlying religious "belief in a God of justice who operates a lawful universe, punishing and rewarding according to principles of proportion, mercifully mitigated in exceptional cases."[1] In the twentieth century, however, this historical connection between law and its religious roots has been substantially broken. This erosion of its historical foundations constitutes the real crisis of modern law.

Berman's study is primarily analytical rather than constructive. The secular and increasingly global context of present-day law precludes the possibility of return to the legal systems of the past. Nevertheless, a study of the tradition is an essential preparation for the constructive task which lies ahead. Such a study reveals the distinctive character of modern Western law: objectivity and universality, rationality, reciprocity, participation, integration, and a capacity for organic growth and development.[2] These qualities were dependent, Berman believes, upon the theological presuppositions underlying the development of canon law (1050–1200), which constitutes the first modern legal system. In a broad sense, these theological convictions were generally shared in the West until the beginning of the twentieth century. During this time secular law was grounded in appeals to the divine law (revealed in Scripture) and natural law and, more recently, in human rights. Today, however, secular law, bereft of its original foundation, is left "suspended, so to speak, in mid-air."[3]

Though the religious basis of the legal tradition has eroded, the story of the development of the latter provides an indispensable historical perspective for the creation of new forms of law in a secular, pluralistic and international society. Such a narrative provides insight into the processes by which the foundations were laid for a unified, objective, universal system of law in the West and how that system evolved through times of revolutionary change. Indeed, in the period that lies ahead, Western law may well serve as a new "corpus juris Romani" for the development of a common legal language and the formation of a new legal order for all humankind, an order that is both stable and just.[4] The study of Western law will need to be supplemented, however, by similar attention to non-Western legal systems and traditions; for they, too, are indispensable participants in the creation of a global community of order and justice. They, too, will provide critical texts for the development of a common legal language and the creation of new forms of legal order.

Berman's study is particularly pertinent to the present examination of justice for a number of reasons. First, Berman calls attention to the manner in which the legal system of the West has been shaped by a variety of traditions, including especially Greek and Roman law and the biblical understanding of God's justice, as well as the customary laws of different peoples. Each of these traditions contained certain critical texts which have been rediscovered, reappropriated, and applied in new circumstances. These texts became important components of the developing legal system. In the course of rediscovery and reappropriation, the texts themselves – the traditions which they symbolized – were mutually reinterpreted and transformed. This process of retrieval and reinterpretation continues into the present.

Secondly, Berman's study of the development of Western law points to the presence of a deeply rooted pluralism in that tradition from the beginning. This pluralism was expressed not only in terms of the duality between secular and ecclesiastical systems of law, but also in terms of a pluralism of largely autonomous secular legal systems. To be sure, acceptance of such forms of pluralism between ecclesiastical and secular jurisdictions and especially among national states was based upon the common acknowledgment of an objective and universal moral order grounded in the divine will. Under such circumstances the question of pluralism was ultimately transcended through confidence in the creative and ordering activity of a just and sovereign God. Today, however, the problem of pluralism arises at a far more fundamental level, namely, the erosion of the religious foundation of the entire Western legal tradition. The alternatives to order based on justice are subjectivism (fragmentation of community), order based upon coercion (power), and positivism.

In the third place, Berman's concept of the interaction of law and religion points to the dynamic character of the relationship between the two. On the one hand, law and religion are independent realities, each with its own identity and history so that neither is reducible to the other; yet, on the other hand, they are also mutually interdependent so that neither can be fully understood in isolation from the other. Each is most adequately comprehended in terms of a tradition which includes more than a body of rules (law) or a system of beliefs (religion); each also includes the expression of such rules or beliefs in practice. Like religion, law "involves not only reason and will but also emotion, intuition, faith."[5]

Law and religion are primarily concerned with different relationships. Law in the secular sense has to do principally with life in the "earthly city." Its goal is the provision of order and justice in human communities. In contrast, in its Judaic and Christian forms, religion is principally concerned with humanity's relationship to God. Humanity's proper relationship to God includes both the exclusive worship of, and final obedience to, God. Yet, while the relationships involved in law and religion may be thus sharply distinguished for purposes of analysis, they are not mutually exclusive. The first requirement of prophetic religion is to love God with all of one's heart, soul, mind, and strength; and the second is to love one's neighbor as oneself (Mark 12:28:31; cf. Deut.6:5 and Lev.19:18). As previously noted, law is in turn grounded ultimately in certain fundamentally religious convictions which provide the basis for belief in a moral order that is rational, objective, universal, and dynamic. Berman describes this ongoing pattern of relationships between law and religion variously in terms of mutual interaction, dialectical tension, and transformation.

In the fourth place, Berman's developmentalist interpretation of the growth of the Western legal system implies a relational conception of law and justice. This does not mean that law and justice are therefore subjective. In the debate between legal formalism and policy-oriented forms of legal reasoning, Berman's sympathies clearly are much closer to the former than the latter.[6] The answer to an excessive emphasis upon logical consistency in the law is not an attack upon the general rules of law and justice but rather "a balance among rule, precedent, polity, and equity."[7] Such a balance has been struck in the Western legal tradition, and an attack upon any one of these four elements tends to diminish the others and threaten the system as a whole. In the name of antiformalism, a "public policy" approach to law tends to view law as "wholly contingent, contemporary, and arbitrary." As an alternative both to rigid formalism and to "public policy" forms of legal reasoning, Berman stresses "the autonomy, the integrity, and the ongoingness" of the legal tradition itself. In this tradition, law and justice are viewed as objective, rational, and universal; as such, they stand in judgment upon all historical political systems.

Such a relational conception of law is implicit in the process of adaptation of Western law to different forms of positive law from the Papal Revolution of the eleventh and twelfth centuries onward. It is evident more particularly in the acknowledged legitimacy of pluralistic forms of secular law, not only within nation states but across national boundaries. Law involves custom and equity, not just statutes and court decisions.[8] Particularly in its earlier, formative era, Western law was derived largely from custom, which was interpreted in the light of equity (reason and conscience). For Berman, law is a *process* of interpretation and application of general rules in the light of particular institutions, procedures, values, and patterns of thought. Thus understood, law involves reciprocity, participation, and growth.[9] It is subject to reinterpretation and new forms of application as evidenced, for example, by evolving and changing conceptions of social justice and human rights.

A STUDY IN THEOLOGICAL ETHICS

The present work focuses upon one aspect of the relations of law to religion, namely, the question of the meaning and sources of justice. In pursuing this question one is led necessarily to a consideration of justice both from the perspective of religion and from that of law. In Judaism and Christianity, God is just and righteous. Not only is he just in his relationships with human-kind; he also requires justice in the human, earthly community. He rules over all nations, and his judgments and salvation extend to the ends of the earth. Such a concept of the divine justice does not mean, however, that the divine will is revealed primarily in codes of religious and civil law. Belief in a God who demands justice does not so much provide an answer to the concrete meaning of justice in the secular realm as it sets an agenda, gives motivation, and provides a perspective by which all human forms of justice are finally measured. Protest against injustice and the promise of justice are constant themes of biblical faith. They are fundamental elements in the biblical conceptions of the kingdom of God, the messianic hope, and the final judgment.

If one begins, on the other hand, with an examination of justice from the perspective of secular law, one cannot escape the issue of the criteria of justice, particularly of just laws. Moreover, one is brought face to face with the question of the foundations of justice. What is the basis for the claims of justice? What is the source of the obligation to act justly? How is justice related to human fulfillment? Many answers have, of course, been given to such questions in the past, and many are still given today. These include natural law, positivism, and critical skepticism (legal realism). In part, the justifications which have been given for such positions are philosophical; they are also intentionally religious, as in appeals to natural and divine law. In either case, reflection upon the meaning and foundations of legal justice raises issues that go beyond law itself and pose questions about the justice of particular laws and, most importantly, about the final basis of authority of the system itself. The answers to such questions are rooted in underlying conceptions of human nature and the moral order. As such they rest finally upon faith – whether secular or religious – rather than upon empirical data. In this sense, the questions themselves are fundamentally religious in character.

While the following study is interdisciplinary both in intent and in design, it is basically an essay in theological ethics. Its purpose is to provide a basis for the mutual engagement of theology and law in the common task of justice. Historically, Roman Catholicism has provided a language for such a discourse in the form of natural law. Protestantism, on the other hand, has generally rejected the latter as a basis for a social ethic. In contrast to Lutheranism, it should be noted, the Reformed tradition, represented by Calvin and Puritanism, has retained a stronger basis for a modified conception of natural law. On the whole, however, the concept of justice has either been neglected or separated from the work of love in Protestantism. Justice has tended to be understood primarily in terms of obedience to existing institutions, and the maintenance of order in society. Love, on the other hand, has tended to be limited to interpersonal relationships.[10] Where justice has been taken most seriously, it has been interpreted primarily in formalist categories. Adequate attention has not been given either to the relational character of justice or to its social and psychological sources.

The crisis of justice constitutes, therefore, one of the most fundamental crises not only in law but also in ethics, including both philosophical and theological forms of the latter. Even in Catholic thought, natural law – at least in its traditional usage – no longer proves viable as the basis for secular law in a pluralistic age.[11] Attempts to address the problem of justice in the present day lead inevitably to the reality of pluralism. Confronted with pluralism, Alasdair MacIntyre suggests that the quest for justice has been replaced by struggles for power in modern society. This is true, he believes, because society has lost that underlying sense of unity and purpose which alone makes agreement about justice possible. A renewal of justice is therefore dependent upon a rebirth of homogeneous moral communities based upon a common narrative and a shared moral vision.[12] Although the contemporary crisis of Western law is unprecedented in its depth, Berman seems less pessimistic about the prospects of pluralism, perhaps because the story of Western law includes an account of the ways in which less radical forms of pluralism have been incorporated into the tradition itself. Others, including Milner Ball, Michael Walzer, and Donald Lutz find in the biblical image of covenant a contemporary metaphor for understanding political community and law.[13] In the pages which follow, attention will be given to the resources which the traditions of virtue, natural law, and covenant provide for dealing with the problem of justice in a pluralistic society. Throughout, an attempt will be made to bring philosophical and political writers into conversation with theologians and ethicists about the nature, sources, and criteria of justice. Such an approach to the contemporary problem seems promising since it follows a pattern which is present in the historical development of Western law and theology.

METHOD OF INQUIRY

While the study is normative and constructive in its intent, its method is basically phenomenological. An effort will be made, first of all, to identify the moral dimensions, or components, and the underlying structures of justice as these appear in certain major traditions – or "texts" – which have deeply influenced our contemporary thinking about justice. Aristotle is particularly helpful in this regard on account of the method which he employs in analyzing moral experience. In the *Nicomachean Ethics* Aristotle speaks of four dimensions of justice: just person, just acts, just laws, and transcendent justice. All are included in the common idea of justice. In addition, he describes certain fundamental structures of community life, each of which is related to a corresponding form of justice. First, there are the relationships of individuals to one another (reciprocal or exchange justice). Secondly, there are the relationships which the community as a whole has to its individual members (distributive justice). Finally, there are the relationships which individuals have to the community as a whole (general justice). Through Aquinas the ethics of Aristotle were incorporated into traditional Catholic moral thought as part of a synthesis of reason and revelation.

Although the interpretations of justice in the ensuing chapters do not generally use Aristotle's terminology as their primary language, they nevertheless deal with the same basic dimensions and structures of justice. A major purpose of the present inquiry is to examine the specific forms in which both the continuities and the differences between the various traditions appear. The task itself is twofold. It includes an investigation of the primary metaphors in each tradition; but it also includes an exploration of the extent to which the primary images of each tradition are supplemented or reinforced by secondary images which are present in the moral language of the community as a whole.[14]

Analysis of the structures of justice points to the underlying relationships in which the claims of justice are grounded. The structures of justice constitute basic patterns of interaction of the self with others. As such, they are present in all collective forms of human life. In the chapters which follow, we will encounter sharp differences regarding the nature and substantive claims of justice in the various texts which will be examined. An investigation of the underlying human relationships provides a framework for analyzing not only the differences but also the commonalities among these traditions. Such a study will help to clarify the historical relationships between these traditions; it also points to their continued presence and mutual interaction in Western society. Clearly, they cannot be reduced to a single idea of justice without losing much of their individual richness and vitality. Rather, their relationships to each other are best understood in dialogical or dialectical terms. Together they contribute to the renewal and transformation of justice in modern, pluralistic forms of society. By focusing upon the forms of justice in human experience, we are able to see more clearly the relationship between beliefs and values, being and doing, rules and virtue, reason and the affections both in moral agency and in the fulfillment of human life in community.

Certain common questions run through all of the ensuing chapters. The following in particular are especially pertinent to the present inquiry: is justice understood primarily in terms of virtue? If so, does it include certain rules or laws as well? Conversely, if justice is perceived primarily in terms of law, does it likewise entail some notion of virtue? If justice includes both virtue and law, how are the two ideas related? Does the idea of justice presuppose some essentially religious referent in terms of which all systems of positive justice are finally judged? If such a transcendent norm is presupposed, how is it understood, and what relationship does it bear to historical forms of justice?

PROCEDURE

Taking a cue form Berman, the procedure of the present essay will be to examine selected traditions or "texts" which have been historically influential in the formation and shaping of the Western tradition of justice. Separate chapters are devoted to the classical tradition of virtue (Aristotle and Aquinas), the biblical conception of God's righteousness, the idea of covenant in Puritanism, and Locke's theory of social compact. Chapter six is a case study of the moral foundations of the American Republic. The concluding chapter represents an attempt to provide a theological interpretation of the relations of justice to law based upon a covenantal understanding of community.

Understood in terms of covenant, justice is perceived fundamentally as promise. A covenantal conception of community provides the basis for an affirmation of pluralism rooted theologically in Creation and the divine ordering of human life. In this context, the relationship between theology and secular systems of justice is dialectical and interactive. It involves a process of mutual transformation. Covenantal justice is relational and developmental, rather than formal and static. It also implies participation of all members of the political community in the determination of particular forms of civil justice and public policy.

CHAPTER 2

The classical tradition of virtue

The present work is a study in the nature and meaning of justice in theological ethics. More particularly, it is concerned primarily with the relations of justice to virtue and law. In view of the renewed attention to virtue both in theological and in philosophical ethics, we turn, first, to the attempt to define justice fundamentally in terms of virtue. Do writers in the tradition of virtue themselves maintain that justice can be adequately understood as virtue, or do they also appeal to certain rules – or laws – to establish criteria of justice in human communities? If justice includes both law and virtue, how are the latter ideas related? Finally, how is the demand for justice ultimately grounded? Is justice, indeed, a viable concept in modern pluralistic society?

JUSTICE BASED ON VIRTUE

In an effort to explore these questions we begin with three contemporary ethicists who have attempted to ground morality in public life fundamentally upon the notion of virtue. The first of these writers – Alasdair MacIntyre – is a philosopher; the remaining two – Stanley Hauerwas and James M. Gustafson – are theologians. While each is deeply influenced by Aristotle and Aquinas, all three fail to give adequate attention to the relation of justice to law both in Aristotle and Aquinas, but particularly in Aquinas. The ensuing section of the present chapter is devoted to an analysis of the structures of justice as a requirement of collective forms of human life. Consideration of the structures of justice leads, in turn, to the question of the relationship of justice to law. Finally, attention is given to the relationship of justice to other virtues such as equity, friendship, and charity.

In *After Virtue* Alasdair MacIntyre presented a provocative critique of morality in modern society and a deeply pessimistic appraisal of the prospect for the renewal of public morality. In pronouncing the demise of virtue, including the virtue of justice, MacIntyre raised the question of whether justice is a meaningful concept in the modern world. He traced the crisis in contemporary morality – both public and private – to the period of the Enlightenment, during which time the classical tradition of virtue (Aristotle and the Middle Ages) was replaced by individualistic conceptions of human nature and emotivist conceptions of morality. These changes reflected the loss of an underlying sense of community based upon the pursuit of a common good. In the tradition of virtue not only was the practice of virtue intrinsically good for individual moral agents; it also nurtured the community in its pursuit of the well-being of the whole.

The absence of such an underlying sense of community in modern society is evident in the replacement of virtue with rights and rules in moral philosophy, in the rise of contract theories of society, and in the growing disjunction between law and morality. The loss of a theological concept of essential human nature resulted in the advent of autonomous moral agents, and in the divorce of the rules of morality from their grounding in essential human nature and divine law. All subsequent efforts to provide a new basis for traditional rules – notably utilitarianism (Bentham and Mill) and formalism (Kant) – have failed because they are basically individualistic and abstracted from the practice of virtue by which moral communities are ultimately sustained and nurtured.

While all of these changes affected the quality of both private and public life, their effect upon the latter is most directly evident in the changing conceptions of justice as a virtue. For Aristotle, justice was the first virtue of political life; moreover, practical agreement concerning the nature of justice was prerequisite for political community.[1]

Though justice was fundamentally a virtue, as such it needed to be supplemented by laws which prohibited certain kinds of

actions which were antithetical to justice.[2] Nevertheless, the rules
of justice remained subordinated to justice as a virtue in two
important respects. In the first place, virtue was the primary
concept so that the rules of justice were finally derived from
justice as a virtue; and, in the second place, only the person who
possesses the virtue of justice knows how to apply the rules. Most
importantly, for Aristotle the political community was a moral
community, a community in which law and morality were united.
Harmony between the well-being of the individual and that of the
community was presupposed.

In contrast with the Greek city states and medieval Christendom, modern society is characterized by pluralism and
conflict over individual rights and duties. As a whole it possesses
no unifying narrative, and its members are committed to no
common practice in the pursuit of a common end. Agreement
about justice as the central virtue of political communities has
been replaced by debates about the rules of justice and
individual rights. In the absence of agreement about the nature
and significance of virtue, conflicts concerning the rules of
justice seem irresolvable. The tragedy and the precariousness of
our contemporary culture lie in the fact that, lacking any
agreement about justice as virtue, no agreement about the rules
of justice is possible. Justice as a virtue in the classical sense has
been replaced by concepts of distributive justice (Rawls) and
justice as entitlement (Nozick). Disputes between such disparate
claims cannot be resolved apart from the recovery of the
tradition of virtue. So long as such a tradition is lacking, no
"genuine moral consensus" is possible, and modern politics will
remain a form of civil war.[3] Like the Roman Empire, our
culture has declined into a period of the new "dark ages."[4] It
has reached a decisive turning point in the struggle of the
Aristotelian tradition against the onslaught of liberal individualism. Yet we are not entirely devoid of hope, for just as the
tradition of the virtues led to the construction of new forms of
community within which civility and the intellectual and moral
life could be sustained through the earlier dark ages, so now
the times call for the construction of similar local forms of
community in which morality and virtue can be sustained and

nurtured during the new age of barbarism which is upon us. In
this sense we are waiting for another – but doubtless a very
different – St. Benedict.[5]

MacIntyre leaves us finally with a double morality based upon
our relationship to two different communities, one ruled by law
and one by virtue. The tradition of the virtues implies "a rejection
of the modern political order";[6] yet, many tasks which need to be
performed in our society can only be performed through governmental institutions. The rule of law must be vindicated, injustice
and unwarranted suffering need to be attended to, generosity
must be exercised, and liberty defended. Each particular task,
each particular responsibility, will need to be "evaluated on its
own merits."[7] Precisely what this means in terms of the moral
criteria of public policy is unclear. Justice in the tradition of virtue
is systematically rejected by modern political institutions. Apparently, only rules of justice remain, but there is no rational way to
adjudicate between the competing rules. True morality, however,
exists only in local forms of community based upon a shared
narrative and upon the practice of virtue in the pursuit of a
common goal.

MacIntyre has provided a forceful analysis of the conflict
between liberal individualism and the claims of communities in
modern Western society. This conflict is rooted in the demise of
political communities built upon the tradition of virtue. Conflicts
between the good of individuals and that of the polis were not
possible in that tradition, for the fulfillment of both consisted in
the pursuit of a common goal. But in modern societies, such
conflicts are inevitable and irresolvable on a moral basis due to
the rise of contractualist forms of society based upon claims of
individual liberties and rights.

MacIntyre's proposal for the formation of local forms of
community in which the practice of virtue can be nurtured and
sustained is important; as an answer to the problem of justice,
however, it is finally inadequate, for it makes such a problem
basically irrelevant in modern, pluralistic societies. This inadequacy is due in part at least to his narrow conception of virtue (his
neglect of public virtue), his derivation of law from virtue, and his
negative appraisal of pluralism. For MacIntyre, moral selfhood is

defined in terms of a narrative quest for the good, a quest which is shared both by individuals and by the community as a whole. It is in the context of such a quest that moral selves are formed and the moral life is understood in terms of agency, intelligibility, and mutual accountability.[8]

In *Whose Justice? Which Rationality?* MacIntyre provides the basis for a potentially more positive assessment of pluralism than he does in *After Virtue*.[9] Here he is more open to dialogue among the traditions. He cites the Thomistic dialectical synthesis of Aristotle and Augustine as an example of the way in which traditions are changed;[10] he also describes the transformation of liberalism into a comparatively new tradition. For MacIntyre, the question of the rationality of justice is always a question of the rationality of particular forms of justice considered in terms of their historical contexts. The various traditions – each based upon its own standards of rationality – are related dialectically to each other. Since there is no neutral, value-free standard for measuring the rationality of the competing systems, the dialectic continues unresolved – unless adherents to one tradition are "converted" to another.[11] In the end, however, MacIntyre's emphasis here – as in *After Virtue* – is upon the "deep incompatibility" between the rational traditions of justice and contemporary modes of debate about justice based upon principles/rules, individual rights, and duties.

Since morality and civility are meaningful and possible for MacIntyre only within the context of communities which share a common moral tradition, it is unclear how personal identity, agency, and accountability can either be understood or embodied in contemporary moral experience. Phenomenologically speaking, however, these characteristics of moral selfhood seem to be embedded more broadly in human experience generally and not exclusively in that of homogeneous groups which share a common story and a common quest. At least during the interim until our contemporary pluralism is replaced by a new universal moral community, the questions of justice and community necessarily include questions of responsibility and accountability in the midst of our given pluralism.

After Virtue is written from the standpoint of moral philosophy rather than theological ethics. Hence, it will be helpful to look briefly at two contemporary writers who have undertaken to interpret Christian ethics primarily in terms of character (Hauerwas) or virtue (Gustafson). In so doing both have been deeply influenced by the understanding of virtue in traditional Catholic thought as well as by more recent studies of the nature and development of the self in psychology, sociology, and moral philosophy.[12]

In *A Community of Character*, Stanley Hauerwas moves toward the development of "a constructive Christian social ethics" based fundamentally upon the notion of character. In contrast to MacIntyre, Hauerwas is concerned with the distinctive quality of Christian ethics and with the role of the church in politics and public policy. Both writers emphasize the importance of narrative and virtue in ethics. Whereas MacIntyre finds the unity of the moral life in the narrative of the agent, Hauerwas locates it in the character of the self. For both, "integrity" understood in terms of the fundamental story of the self becomes the ultimate norm of moral decisions, including, in particular, tragic choices. Although he agrees with MacIntyre that the cultivation of a life of virtue presupposes a community which shares a common narrative and a common tradition, for theological reasons Hauerwas attributes greater value to pluralism.[13] For him the church is fundamentally a religious moral community which knows and proclaims the true story about the meaning of human life and history, that is, the story of the Kingdom of God.[14] Not only does this story provide the basis for a distinctively Christian ethic based upon the religious beliefs of the Christian community; it also provides the basis for a true understanding of the secular world.

The church lives in a pluralistic culture, and its primary task in relation to that culture is to exist as the church.[15] Its first responsibility is to live out its own story – a deeply social and political story – and to tell this story to the world to provide people with "categories of interpretation" for a proper understanding of themselves. While Hauerwas' conception of the relationship of the church to culture most closely resembles H. Richard Niebuhr's "Christ Against Culture" type, he rejects the "withdrawal" of the church from culture.[16] According to

Hauerwas, the church exists wherever people faithfully witness to the reality of God's Kingdom.[17] Since this reality is a social reality and since God rules over the kingdoms of this world, the church must address the world, and Christians must participate in the social and political life of their time. Hauerwas' emphasis, however, is upon the essential moral opposition between the church and the world based upon the different narratives in terms of which the two understand themselves. The church must be in the world. By being faithful to its Lord in the midst of the world, it may convert outsiders to its own story and its distinctive ethos; there is little hope for the transformation of institutions except perhaps the family. The responsibility of the church is to be the "sacramental sign" of the Kingdom of God as the community of reconciliation.[18] The church serves society best by forming a people who have "the virtues and trust necessary to sustain a polity capable of maintaining a rich pluralism of differences."[19] Understood in terms of God's creation, the world of culture is good although it is sinful, and pluralism is part of God's design for the enrichment of human history.

Yet Hauerwas fails to provide an adequate theological basis for constructive Christian social ethics. He criticizes John Howard Yoder for his inability to appreciate the positive achievements of political community based on "mutual trust and aspiration for the good."[20] Christians must use the language of justice if they are to make any discriminating social judgments; however, it is their task to transform the language of justice by relating it to Christ. Seen from this perspective, justice is incompatible with the use of violence.[21] Hauerwas is also critical of Reinhold Niebuhr's political realism.[22] This mode of politics, he contends, reduces justice to a procedure which requires only the balancing of competing interests. Such a view neglects the possibilities of substantive justice and the common good for the creation of a good society. Hence Hauerwas seeks to recover the meaning of community in politics through a revival of the notion of a common good. Such a notion would be arrived at through public deliberation about collective goals and common actions rather than the special interests of competing groups. Ironically at this point, however, Hauerwas is unable to integrate the resources of natural justice and the common good into his social ethics because he does not have an adequate doctrine of creation. As a result, "the church has little to offer in terms of political strategy." Its primary task is "to become a polity that has the character necessary to survive as a truthful society."[23] The work of justice is necessary in human history, but this is not the church's task. The church's main contribution to justice lies in the formation of a people informed by certain virtues (chief among which are hope and patience), capable of witnessing to God's truth in the world.[24]

Whereas Hauerwas interprets Christian ethics as an ethics of character, James M. Gustafson interprets it primarily in terms of virtue. As noted above, both ethicists are strongly influenced by the tradition of virtue in Aristotle and Aquinas. Hauerwas, however, emphasizes the distinctiveness of Christian ethics based upon God's revelation in Christ and the particularity of the Christian story. For him, as for MacIntyre, the first moral question is: "Of what history am I a part and how can I best understand it?"[25] For Hauerwas this story is fundamentally a Christological story, that is, the story of Jesus. "Character" refers to the basic orientation, or perspective, of the self. It signifies the "distinctive style" which characterizes all of a person's traits and activities; it refers to the identity and integrity of the agent and accounts for the consistency in that person's behavior.[26] The virtues, on the other hand, refer to more specific traits such as honesty or kindness or justice. Character signifies a more fundamental determination of the self than do the virtues; moreover, the virtues receive their particular form through the character of the agent.

In contrast to Hauerwas, Gustafson states the primary question of theological ethics as follows: "What is God enabling and requiring us to be and to do?"[27] This formulation of the basic question presupposes the creation of a moral order to which individuals and institutions ought to conform. In many respects, Gustafson's ethics represent an effort to construct a synthesis of morality based on reason, and morality based on revelation.[28] This understanding of the relationship of nature to grace provides the basis for a modified form of natural law. As in Catholicism, the latter idea is closely associated with a teleological conception of God's relationship to the world, a teleological (purposive) conception of moral agency, and a tradition in which virtue is integrally related to moral choice.

Whereas Hauerwas defines character primarily in terms of the agent's fundamental perspective, Gustafson uses the concept in a more general sense to include the agent's beliefs, dispositions, affections, and intentions and, particularly, the manner in which these are interrelated in persons.[29] Gustafson's conception of character is broader than that of Hauerwas, and it is more deeply rooted in natural law. Character is set within the larger framework of an ethic of virtue which, at least in its classical Catholic form, has traditionally provided a more objective and a generalized basis for moral claims. For Gustafson, however, the objective and universal elements in moral judgments are grounded historically in human experience rather than ontologically in the order of being. Critical analysis of moral experience provides the basis for the development of action-guiding principles, or general rules, and the prioritizing of ends and values.[30] For Christians, such principles and values are inferences, first of all, from the religious beliefs of Christians; but, for the most part, they can also be stated in broadly human – that is, natural and rational – terms, and they can be justified on rational grounds.[31]

The development of such norms is a communal task. It involves interpretation both of the meaning of Christian faith and of contemporary events in the light of this faith. As a task for the community, it presupposes the existence of moral communities which function in two ways. Firstly, they are needed to provide contexts for the nurture of virtue and the formation of character. Secondly, they are also needed as occasions for moral discourse and the praxis of moral reasoning. Particularly in dealing with complex societal issues in a pluralistic setting, communities of moral discourse need to be representative of the larger community as a whole, in order that different moral points of view may be included. They also need to include specialists in various legal, medical, economic, and environmental dimensions of such problems as well as administrators charged with the responsibility for final decisions and their implementation in these matters. The purpose of such discourse is to broaden and deepen understanding of the problems at hand, including both their technical and moral dimensions. In this way such communities contribute to the formation of policy in the public arena.[32]

Like Calvin, Gustafson makes "the third use of the law" – that is, its pedagogical function – the principal one. The quest for "almost absolute" and "almost universal" principles and values is necessary in order to give specificity to the good in human action. Nevertheless, obedience to law remains subordinate to virtue. Like duty and law, virtue also provides continuity and direction in moral experience; at the same time it allows for greater human autonomy in the pursuit of the well-being and fulfillment of creation. Just as the virtues describe the "moral requisites" for personal human fulfillment, so they also define the conditions which are necessary for the existence and nurture of human community.[33] As the theological virtues (faith, hope, and love) are necessary for the sustenance and fulfillment of human life in interpersonal relations, so they along with many others are also essential for the enrichment of human community. Other virtues which are requisite for both personal and communal forms of human life include freedom, justice, and order.[34] Although he recognizes the need for rules and law, Gustafson has, up to this point at least, left this aspect of his ethics largely undeveloped. This includes the notion of justice.

Thus far we have been considering the attempt to ground morality in public life on virtue. According to MacIntyre, the substance of morality in its communal dimensions depends in particular on the fate of justice understood as a virtue.[35] The tradition of virtue includes "rules of justice" as well as virtue; however, the former are derived from the latter. Since contemporary society is not shaped by a common moral tradition, it lacks the necessary basis for communal justice. Hauerwas agrees largely with MacIntyre's analysis of the nature and sources of community. For him, Christian ethics has little to contribute to the development of political strategy and the formation of public policy; moreover, Hauerwas appears to provide even less of a place for rules than MacIntyre. Although Gustafson provides a broader basis for the development of rules of justice in a historicized conception of natural law, he has not as yet under-taken such an analysis of justice.

In order to provide a basis for testing the adequacy of justice as a virtue, it will be helpful to look briefly at the structures of justice as a requirement of collective forms of human life.

Whether it is understood primarily in terms of virtue or in terms of rules or principles, justice is concerned fundamentally with relationships with "the other." For Aristotle, justice is distinguished from all of the remaining virtues in that it alone is directed toward "the good of others"; it "promotes the interests of somebody else."[36] According to Georgio Del Vecchio, the greatest merit of the Aristotelian theory of justice lies in its grasp of *alteritas* as "the fundamental and specific significance of justice."[37] That Aristotle did not draw out the full implications of this insight was due in part at least to the presence in his thought of two different concepts of justice, namely, general (legal) justice and particular (juridical) justice.

As the comprehensive form of justice, legal justice is "an exercise of complete virtue"; it is "the whole of virtue."[38] It is not, however, merely the sum of all of the virtues; rather, it enlarges the *telos* of the practice of virtue to include the well-being of others and not simply of oneself. General justice and virtue refer to the same moral state. When this moral state is considered "relative to others," it is termed justice; when it is considered "absolutely as a moral state," it is called virtue.

In Aristotle's investigation of particular justice the distinctive quality of justice becomes clearer. Particular justice is a part of general justice, but it is concerned primarily with relationships with other persons. Particular justice means fairness or equality in the treatment of others; it is fundamentally concerned with the notion of desert. It means giving "to each according to his or her due." Here again Aristotle distinguishes between two kinds of particular justice, one of which he calls "distributive" and the other "corrective" or retributive. Distributive justice refers to the apportionment of the goods of a community (such as wealth and honor) among its members on the basis of their merit. As Aristotle notes: "[E]verybody admits that justice in distributions is determined by merit of some sort; only people do not understand the same thing by merit. The democrats understand freedom, the oligarchs wealth or nobility, and the aristocrats virtue."[39] Distributive justice is proportional. Corrective justice, on the other hand, has to do with relationships between individuals; it is concerned with fairness in their private transactions. Its aim is the restoration of a prior state of equilibrium between loss and gain in mutual exchange. Aristotle describes this form of justice as an arithmetical mean between profit and loss.

Putting aside the ambiguities and limitations of Aristotle's account of justice as a whole, his analysis of the fundamental form of justice has been a major contribution to the understanding of justice in Western culture. Following Aristotle, Aquinas also defined justice as that virtue which is directed toward others. "Justice, properly so called, regards the duty of one man to another, but all of the other virtues regard the duty of the lower powers to reason."[40] Aquinas also speaks of justice both as a general virtue (the embodiment of all virtue) and as a particular virtue. That justice which directs persons toward others considered as individuals is particular justice. That justice which directs persons toward others as belonging to the community is general, or legal, justice.[41] As the whole of virtue, general justice orders human life toward the common good.[42] Such justice is called legal justice since this direction takes place through law. Legal justice is pre-eminent among the moral virtues inasmuch as the common good surpasses the individual good of a single person.[43] Considered as a particular virtue alongside other virtues, justice orders relationships between individuals in terms of what is due to each.[44]

Drawing upon the Aristotelian–Thomistic analysis of justice, Josef Pieper describes three fundamental structures of communal life which correspond to three basic forms of justice.[45] All three forms of justice, it should be noted, have common qualities. Each has to do with relations to "the others."[46] Each involves recognition of some kind of indebtedness either between individuals or between individuals and the community as a whole. In each instance, moreover, justice is realized primarily in external acts rather than in an inner disposition of the agent. Nevertheless, there are important differences among the three forms of justice, differences which are rooted in the underlying relationships upon which they rest. We turn, therefore, to a brief consideration of the fundamental structures of communal life and their corresponding forms of justice.

First, there are the relations of individuals to one another. The basic form of justice which corresponds to the relationship between individuals is reciprocal, or mutually exchanged, justice. Here the act of justice which orders the relationships of individuals with one another takes the form of restitution or recompense for what is due each person. It is the reinstatement or restoration of an "equilibrium" between persons based on compensation by each for what is due to the other party in the mutual exchange of goods. Such justice is also called compensatory, or commutative, justice.

Secondly, there are the relations of the community as a whole to its individual members. Here the typical community which Pieper, following Aquinas and Aristotle, has in mind is the political community. The basic form of justice which corresponds to the relations of the community as a whole to its individual members is distributive justice. Distributive justice means the proportionate division of the goods which the community possesses in common among its members. It means taking the common good into consideration as the supreme good both of the community and of its individual members and, at the same time, giving to each member that share in the realization of that good which "is due to" each.[47] While there is an implicit notion of individual rights underlying the appeal to "what is due" each member of the community, the traditional doctrine of distributive justice points primarily to the obligation of the ruler to honor the claims of justice rather than to the rights of the claimants themselves.[48]

Finally, there are the relations of individuals to the community as a whole. The basic form of justice which orders the members' relations to the social whole is legal, or general, justice. Pieper does not develop this form of communal

relations and its corresponding structure of justice in any detail.
Presumably, however, he follows Aquinas and Aristotle in this
regard as he does in his treatment of the other two forms of
justice. It will be recalled that for Aquinas general justice
orders human life toward a common good. Legal justice is
general justice expressed in terms of obedience to laws. Like
general justice, legal justice also includes the whole of virtue.
As previously noted, legal justice is not simply an additional
virtue alongside other virtues; on the contrary, it gives to the
latter an element of "otherness." Legal justice does not exist
separately from compensatory and distributive justice; rather, it
prompts the just person to seek for the other what everyone
seeks for his or her self in these as in every form of virtue.[49]
To the extent and in whatever ways the members of a
community contribute to the realization of the common good,
they participate also in the work of legal justice. Clearly, the
particular forms which legal justice may take are dependent
upon the forms of government of particular states. The
possibilities and responsibilities of participation in the political
processes of government are obviously far greater in modern
democratic societies than under authoritarian regimes. This fact
has important implications for understanding the relationship of
justice to law in pluralistic societies.

MORAL COMPONENTS OF JUSTICE

Not only is justice directed toward others; it also presupposes
some concept of "the due, the right, the *suum*."[50] Examination of
this normative, transcendent element in justice will help clarify
both the importance and the limitations of justice as a virtue.
Analysis of this underlying concept of the right involves consideration of three distinct but interrelated components of justice
considered as a moral relationship. These elements are the just
agent, just acts, and just rules.

For Aristotle justice refers, first of all, to the moral state of the
agent. Justice means "the moral state which makes people
capable of doing what is just, and which makes them just in
action and in intention."[51] As such, justice is contrasted with

injustice, that is, with that moral state which makes people unjust in action and intention. Justice is basically what the just person does; nevertheless, Aristotle observes that it is possible for a just person to commit an unjust act.[52] Insofar as justice refers to the moral state of the agent, it is primarily a settled disposition to treat others equally or fairly. Yet a just person, acting out of passion, may commit an unjust act such as adultery or theft without having any defect of moral purpose. In order to comprehend the full meaning of justice as a moral state it is necessary not only to distinguish between just and unjust persons but also between persons and their actions.

Political justice in particular raises the question of the relation of justice to rules or laws. While political justice is closely related to general justice, the former refers more specifically to the laws of particular states. In this context justice means conformity to positive law. It means doing what is lawful. Significantly, however, at this point Aristotle introduces a distinction between political justice that is based on nature and that which is based on convention.[53] Natural justice is universal in its authority; it is independent of opinion. Conventional justice, on the other hand, is determined by the laws and customs of particular states. While there may be only immutable justice among the gods, in this world all justice is mutable and contingent. "Nevertheless, there is a justice which is, as well as a justice which is not, natural."[54] Although the rules of justice and forms of polity may vary according to convention, there is "only one naturally perfect polity."

Aristotle's analysis of the foregoing components of justice is useful in so far as it points to three distinct but interrelated aspects of justice. Indeed, our primary interest in turning to his analysis of justice has been a concern with the forms of justice which he describes rather than the particular moral criteria which he presupposes. In *Politics* there is a fuller development of the function of law in political community. Here Aristotle suggests three important ways in which law is related to justice. Firstly, law is needed in ordering the members of a political community toward a common end. Laws are necessary in all forms of government; when the former are good, they should be

supreme.[55] Secondly, law has an indispensable function in the
education of the members of a community, particularly its
youth.[56] Finally, although he does not provide a basis for
transcending the limitations of the Greek city-state, Aristotle
raises the issue of a transcendent justice by which the laws of
particular states are measured. On the one hand, the positive law
determines what is just; yet, on the other hand, some laws are
manifestly unjust.

Significantly, all of the foregoing elements – the just person, the
just act, and just law, together with a concept of "right" that is
presupposed – are present in Aquinas' synthesis of Aristotelian
and Christian ethics. In reference to the moral agent, justice is
"the habit whereby a person with a lasting and constant will
renders to each his due."[57] Just actions are actions which conform
to right reason.[58] The proper activity of justice is "to render to
each his own."[59] Finally, Aquinas sets the question of legal justice
in the context of a four-fold pattern of law wherein human law is
judged in terms of the natural law and ultimately in terms of the
divine law as the highest disclosure of the eternal law.

While Aquinas adopts the basic features of Aristotle's analysis
of justice as a moral relationship, he reinterprets Aristotle in light
of revelation. For Aquinas, humanity has an eternal destiny which
transcends its temporal end; and the moral virtues are supplemented and qualified by the theological virtues, particularly by
charity. Our present concern, however, is not with the different
content which Aquinas gives to justice in contrast to Aristotle;
rather, our purpose has been to show how in both of these
classical forms of ethics based on virtue, consideration of justice
entails consideration of three distinctive albeit complementary
aspects of justice – the just agent, the just rule, and the just act.[60]
A full understanding of justice includes all three of these components. Moreover, as we have seen, each of these presupposes
some notion of "the due" or "the right."[61]

THE INSUFFICIENCY OF JUSTICE

Before turning to a consideration of justice in the biblical teaching
of God's righteousness, attention should be directed to one

additional aspect of justice in the classical tradition, namely, the relationship of justice to other virtues. While justice is the first virtue of political communities for Aristotle, it is neither the only nor the sufficient political virtue. Aristotle defines legal justice as obedience to the laws of particular states. In the application of such laws, however, he appeals to equity in order to rectify legal justice where such a system fails through generality.[62] Equity is a kind of justice and indeed, is superior to some forms of legal justice. Friendship is also an indispensable virtue of political communities; it is the "bond which holds states together."[63] In its highest form, justice "assumes the character of friendship." The supreme form of friendship is possible, however, only among equals, that is, among persons who are alike in virtue and in their love of the good.[64]

Aquinas similarly recognizes that justice by itself is insufficient for the proper ordering of human life.[65] On the one hand, there are certain obligations and debts which due to their very nature can never be adequately fulfilled or paid. The truly just person seeks to overcome this deficiency in justice through the practice of religion, piety, and gratitude.[66] Religion is that special virtue whereby we repay our debt to God; piety, that whereby we pay our debt to our parents or to our country; and gratitude, that whereby we pay our debt to our benefactors. Friendship is also closely related to justice. Although friendship cannot be claimed as "due" another person, it is nevertheless essential for human fulfillment in community. Stated in terms of theological ethics, charity is prerequisite for the achievement of justice. While charity presupposes justice in the sense that "one can give only what is one's own," charity in turn "supplements and completes" justice.[67]

In the next chapter we turn to a consideration of the relations of justice to virtue and law in the covenantal tradition. The theological roots of covenantal thought are found primarily in the biblical conception of God's righteousness and in the Reformed tradition, particularly in Puritanism. Like virtue, covenant also points to the communal nature of human existence. Unlike virtue, however, covenant rests upon a different understanding of human community, including political community. In the virtue tradition, community is based upon the common practice of virtue and a shared vision of a common good; in covenantal thought it is based upon ties of promise and faithfulness to such promises. Like virtue, covenant also points to a transcendent norm in terms of which all human forms of justice are finally measured.

CHAPTER 3

The righteousness of God and human justice

THE THEOCENTRIC CHARACTER OF BIBLICAL FAITH

When one turns to a consideration of justice in the scriptures of Judaism and Christianity, one immediately encounters a radically different perspective from that which appears in Greek moral philosophy. Whereas the moral life is understood primarily as a life of virtue in classical Greek thought, for the Hebrews it is most characteristically portrayed in terms of obedience to God. It must be emphasized at the outset, however, that such obedience is not fundamentally a matter of conformity to a codified system of revealed law; rather, it is a requirement of faithfulness on the part of the people of Israel not only to God but also with one another. While the divine will is typically disclosed in commandments and laws, these are grounded finally in the creating, ordering, and renewing activity of God in history.

In order to comprehend the unfolding biblical idea of justice, we must attempt to understand it, first of all, in its biblical context. Only then will we have a basis for comparing the forms and content of justice in the classical and Hebraic traditions. What do these understandings of justice have in common? How do they differ? Can the biblical concept of justice be reduced to philosophical terms without losing both its distinctive quality and its motivational force?[1] If not, is the possibility of biblical justice limited to a fundamentally sectarian community which shares the biblical story? Otherwise, is the relationship between Aristotelian and biblical justice most adequately expressed in terms of a hierarchical synthesis of reason and revelation? Finally, does the biblical notion of justice provide a basis for the transformation of

29

both conventional and philosophical forms of justice? What would such a transformationist concept of justice entail? Is it viable in a pluralistic age?

The central and most distinctive feature of biblical religion is its growing perception of the sovereignty and righteousness of God. In the earliest stages of Hebrew history, the existence of other gods was presupposed. The religion of the patriarchs was henotheistic. By the time of Moses (ca.1200 BC), however, Israel acknowledged that her worship and allegiance belonged to Yahweh alone (Ex.20:1–6). When the monotheism which was implicit in the religion of Moses came to full expression in Deutero-Isaiah (Is.40–55), that great prophet of the Babylonian exile viewed himself as standing in the tradition of the patriarchs, Moses, and his prophetic forebears. Similarly, in the New Testament, it is the God of Abraham, Isaac, and Jacob whom Jesus worshipped and whose kingdom he proclaimed. Confronted with the charge of subverting the religious traditions of Judaism, Jesus declared that he had come not to destroy, but to fulfill both the law and the prophets (Matt.5:17ff.; 22:34–40).

The developing conceptions of God's power and righteousness are deeply rooted and ultimately united in the idea of the covenant. Indeed, it is impossible to comprehend the power and righteousness of God apart from the covenant, for it is here that the divine sovereignty and the promise of grace are seen to be one. But while the notion of covenant is fundamental to Hebrew religion, it is God rather than the covenant which constitutes the ultimate object of Israel's faith. It is Yahweh who not only established the covenant but also sustains, renews, and finally fulfills it. Covenant provides the basis for hope and confidence toward the future precisely because it rests on the promise of God.

BIBLICAL CONCEPTIONS OF COVENANT

In view of its importance in both the Old and the New Testaments, we turn now to a consideration of the biblical idea of covenant. While a number of covenants between God and the people are described in the Old Testament, all have at least three major characteristics in common.[2] In the first place, they are agreements between parties which are unequal in status. Secondly, God initiates each covenant and stipulates its terms. Each is an expression of the divine grace and power. Thirdly, the people must decide whether or not they will accept the covenant.

Beyond these basic similarities, there are significant differences among the several covenants. Two covenantal forms are particularly important for present purposes. On the one hand, there are the promissory covenants with Noah, Abraham, and David; and, on the other hand, there is the morally obliging covenant at Sinai. In the first of these types, the promised blessing is unconditional; it depends solely upon the divine election. The covenant with Noah (Gen.9:8–17), for example, is one which Yahweh makes with all humankind and, indeed, with "every living creature" throughout all future generations. In it, God promises that the earth will never again be destroyed by a flood, and he establishes the rainbow as a sign of the covenant which he has made. The eating of blood and the taking of human life are forbidden; if these prohibitions are not heeded, the people will be punished, but the covenant itself is "everlasting" (Gen.9:16). In contrast with the universal promise to Noah, the covenant with Abraham (Gen.17:1–21) is limited to a particular people; at the same time its content is specified in more detail. In it, Yahweh promises three things to Abraham: (1) that he and his descendants will become a people; (2) that the land of Canaan will be their possession; and (3) that Yahweh himself "will be their God." Circumcision is the appointed sign of membership in the elected community. In itself, circumcision is a confessional rite which symbolizes membership in the chosen community It is not a condition of election itself.[3] Similarly, in the covenant with David (II Sam.7:14–17; Ps.89:28– 37) God promises to establish the throne and royal lineage of David forever. If Israel sins, she will be chastened for her transgressions; but God's covenant and his loving-kindness will endure forever. They are based upon the divine promise alone.

The second form of covenant is represented preeminently by the compact which Yahweh made with Israel at Sinai (Ex.19:1–24:11).[4] In its present form the Exodus account of the origin of such a covenant dating back to the time of Moses reflects the work of a later editor. While the idea itself probably emerged sometime before the middle of the eighth century BC, it was most fully developed by the Deuteronomic writers of the seventh to the sixth centuries. They expanded the concept and used it to organize and interpret the history of Israel from her beginnings. For them the covenant between Yahweh and Israel was fundamentally a theological concept which symbolized the distinctiveness of Israel's faith and her vocation to be "the people of God."[5]

Unlike the promissory covenants with Noah, Abraham, and David, the covenant between God and Israel was conditional and bilateral. It includes not only Yahweh's announcement of Israel's election to be his people; it also includes Israel's solemn commitment to serve Yahweh alone and to obey his commandments (Ex.24:3–8; 34:10–28; Deut.26:17–19). If Israel is obedient, she will live and prosper (Ex.20:5–6,12; Deut.5:33; 6:3,17–19; 8:1; 11:8–9). If she is unfaithful, on the other hand, not only will she be punished; she will be cast off and destroyed (Deut.6:15; 8:19–20; 28:15–68).

The commandments which are given at Sinai stipulate what God requires of the people of Israel whom he has chosen to be his. Commonly known as the Ten Commandments, they are also called "the ten words" (Hebrew text, Ex.34:28; Deut.4:13; 10:4).[6] As such they are distinguished from the ordinances found in the Book of the Covenant (Ex.20:22–23:33) and from the statutes and ordinances (Deut.12–26). The commandments themselves are preceded by a brief prologue in which God identifies himself as Yahweh, "who brought you out of the land of Egypt, out of the house of bondage" (Ex.20:1–2). The duties which follow fall into two main divisions. The first four describe Israel's duties towards Yahweh; the last six, duties of the people towards one another. Clearly, the first commandment is primary: All of the others are derived fundamentally from it. Not only does Israel's allegiance belong solely to Yahweh; this loyalty includes both cultic and moral requirements.

The commandments in the Decalogue do not constitute a code of law. They are stated, rather, in terms of unconditional obligations, and no sanctions are stipulated for their violation. Moreover, the precise meaning of the key terms is not specified.

What does it mean, for example, to keep the sabbath day "holy"? What does it mean "to kill"? Is all taking of human life categorically forbidden? Since that is evidently not the intention of the commandment, under what circumstances is the taking of such life permitted? Significantly also, all of the commandments save two – sabbath observance and the honoring of one's parents – are stated in negative form. In any event, they must be interpreted; the precise forms in which they are applied will necessarily vary in accordance with changing historical circumstances.[7] Far from being a set of timeless ethical principles or a system of immutable divine laws, the Decalogue is best understood as a set of covenant obligations which permitted – and, indeed, required – a variety of applications in the ongoing life of Israel.[8]

The commandments are addressed both to individuals and to the community. Israel is to be a covenant people. As a nation she is to be faithful and obedient to Yahweh.[9] (Modern individualistic conceptions of human nature were completely foreign to early Hebrew thought.) Individuals and communities exist together. Killing is forbidden because human life has sacred worth. Protection of human life is essential not only for individual members but also for the well-being of the community as a whole.

The giving of the Decalogue is followed by a ritual in which the people make an oath to obey "all the words of Yahweh and all the ordinances" (Ex.24:3–8). Both the commandments (Ex.20:1–17) and "the ordinances" which follow (Ex.21:1–23:33) are included in the covenant which Moses presents to the people and which they, in turn, vow to obey. Their promise is sealed with a sacrificial offering and the sprinkling of blood upon the altar and upon the people.

The pact at Sinai is theocentric. It rests upon the divine initiative, and Yahweh stipulates its terms. He remains sovereign and free. He is to be obeyed because he has shown grace to Israel in her election and deliverance. But there is also respect for human freedom; God does not force himself upon an unwilling people. Initial entry into the covenant is a matter of Israel's choice. Moreover, Israel was left free to develop her own social and cultural life within the limits of her primary allegiance to God.

The commandments are not simply added to the covenant; on the contrary, they are a constituent part of the covenant. In the words of Stamm, "The covenant comes to expression in the commandments; in the context of the covenant, the commandments are the expression of the faithful relationship between persons."[10] The commandments are Israel's "charter of freedom." At the same time, they also define her responsibility as a covenant people.[11] Henceforth, the themes of divine promise and human obligation run like intertwining threads throughout both the Old and the New Testaments. Taken together, they define the distinctiveness of Israel's self-understanding. This distinctiveness lies not only in the exclusivity of her faith in Yahweh but also in the expression of that faith in the common life.

THE RELATION OF COVENANT TO LAW

In the canonical Hebrew Scriptures, the concepts of covenant and law are closely related. The covenant at Sinai provided the basis for the subsequent development of all Israelite law.[12] Thus, it provides a framework for understanding what the law came to mean in Israel. The covenant itself includes both apodictic and casuistic forms of law. Apodictic law consists of categorical injunctions, usually stated in negative terms, without any specifications as to how they are to be implemented. The best-known examples of such legislation are the Ten Commandments. (Other illustrations are found in Ex.20:23; 23:1–2,6. A similar type of law is found in Ex.21:12,15–17; 22:19. The latter stipulations specify the death penalty for smiting, stealing, and lying with a beast. Such laws seem to reflect an understanding of the relationship of God to Israel similar to that which is presupposed in the Decalogue.) Apodictic law is usually stated in the second person singular imperative.

Casuistic law, on the other hand, is procedural (or case) law; it contains precise instructions as to how particular legal issues are to be resolved. Such legislation opens with a citation of the general issue, which is then followed by specific stipulations concerning the application of the general rule to particular cases.

A typical example of such legislation (Ex.21:7–11) deals with the treatment of female slaves. The general rule is stated thus: "When a man sells his daughter as a slave, she shall not go out as the male slaves do" (Ex.21:7). In the verses which follow, the law specifies that her new master must allow her to be redeemed if she does not please him; he has no right to sell her to a foreign people, seeing he has dealt deceitfully with her. Alternatively, if he designates her for his son, he shall treat her as one of his daughters. Or, again, if he takes unto himself another wife, he shall not withhold from the first her food or her clothing or her marital rights. If he fails to fulfill any of these duties toward her, "she shall go free without any money."[13]

Only the apodictic form of law occurs in the Ten Commandments. In the Book of the Covenant (Ex.20:22–23:33), however, casuistic – or procedural – law is predominant, although elements of both are sometimes found together (Ex.21:2–6, 28–32, for example). It is in respect to case law, moreover, that Hebraic legislation most closely resembles the legal codes of other peoples of the ancient Near East.[14] While the Book of the Covenant probably reflects an older form of tribal law, in its present form it constitutes Yahweh's unconditional demand for faithfulness and respect for human life. The making of idols and offering of sacrifices to any gods other than Yahweh are categorically forbidden (Ex.20:23; 22:20). God's requirement of justice for the poor is unqualified (Ex.23:6). Even where the divine demand does not appear explicitly in apodictic form, the covenantal relationship between Yahweh and Israel is frequently reflected in the procedural law itself. As a result of the impact of the covenant, traditional case law undergoes a certain transformation. Illustrations of such a change are found in the laws related to the treatment of slaves (Ex.21:26–27), the oppressed (sojourners, widows, the fatherless), and the poor (Ex.22.21–27).[15] In comparison with the legal codes of surrounding peoples, Israelite law showed greater humanitarianism and a greater respect for human equality. These qualities, which are reflected in the Book of the Covenant, come to much fuller expression in the later Deuteronomistic legislation.

The book of Deuteronomy ostensibly represents a long speech

of Moses to the people of Israel in the land of Moab before they enter Canaan (Deut.1:1–5). In reality, however, it comes from a much later period and is the product of the development of Israelite law over the course of several centuries. The main section of the book (Deut.4:44–30:20) is devoted to Moses' teaching of the law. Properly speaking, this is not a *Codex iuris.* Not only is the law itself set within the context of the covenant between Yahweh and Israel; the former is addressed to the people in a hortatory and sermonic style. Deuteronomy is perhaps best understood as "a book of legal instruction." Its language is not that of law "but that of the heart and conscience."[16] Yahweh yearns "that there were such a heart in the people" that they would fear him and keep his commandments (Deut.5:29). Israel is summoned to love God "with all your heart, and with all your soul, and with all your might" (Deut.6:5). Finally, the entire law – including the commandments, the ordinances, and the statutes – is summarized in the single requirement "to love Jehovah your God, to walk in all his ways, and to cleave unto him" (Deut.11:22). Such obedience cannot be forced; it depends finally upon fellowship, or friendship, with God.[17] Jon D. Levenson captures the meaning of the law for the devout Jew when he writes:

By ascribing all law to Moses, the canonical Pentateuch has made laws into personal commandments ... The Mosaic Torah is ... a means of communion with a loving and personal God. The energy and spiritual power of the Torah flows in no small measure from its insistence on holding these two dimensions, the outer and the inner, the legal and the affective, in a tight unity, refusing to sacrifice the one on the altar of the other.[18]

In comparison with the Exodus account of the Decalogue, the book of Deuteronomy reflects a much more highly developed form of covenantal theology. Here the tradition of God's promises to the patriarchs and that of the Sinai/Horeb covenant are woven together into a single narrative of God's relationship with Israel. While the divine grace clearly underlies the Exodus version of the covenant, in Deuteronomy, Yahweh is explicitly identified as the God of Abraham. The God who had promised a land to the patriarchs is the same God who had brought Israel out of bondage and entered into a covenant with her at Horeb.

Both the Exodus and the Deuteronomic narratives include accounts of the Decalogue (Ex.20:1–17; Deut.5:1–21). Both also include ordinances and statutes along with the Ten Commandments. In both, the unconditional obligations of the Decalogue are accompanied with detailed stipulations for their implementation. In the effort to apply the covenant to the settled agricultural life in Palestine, however, far greater attention is given in Deuteronomy to the development of procedural law than was the case in Exodus.

It is important to notice in this connection that none of the Old Testament collections of law are intended as state law.[19] In no case did their authority rest upon the king. The monarchs were themselves bound by the covenant, including the requirement of obedience to Yahweh (Deut.17:14–20). This subjection of the king to the law was clearly acknowledged by Josiah of Judea when he made the Book of the Covenant, which had been found in the Temple, the basis for a great national reformation in 622–621 BC. After he had assembled the people and read this book aloud to them, both the king and the people entered into a covenant before Yahweh to keep all of the "commandments and ordinances and statutes" which it contained (II Kings 23:1–3). Further evidence that the laws in the Old Testament were not intended as state laws may be adduced from stipulations such as those prohibiting apostasy from Yahweh (Deut.12:2ff.). These injunctions were not intended to apply to other ethnic groups who continued to dwell in the land and had their own cults.[20]

The Deuteronomic law represented an attempt to apply the covenant to the whole range of community life. A tribal confederacy provided the basic communal and institutional structure for the development and transmission of Israelite law. The tribes came together at various cultic centers on a regular basis to renew and affirm the covenant (Deut.27; 31:9–13; Josh.8:30–35; 24). On such occasions the laws were read aloud, and the people pledged anew their allegiance to God and obedience to all his commandments. The legislation itself was developed over the course of centuries, particularly in the towns and villages under the direction of the local priests and Levites. Cultic, ethical, and jurisdictional ordinances are all included together (Deut.12–26). The Deuteronomist thus establishes a strong, internal unity between the cultic and the political ordinances, based upon a profound understanding of the divine love and the divine purpose for Israel. Faithfulness to the covenant includes recognition of the basic dignity and personal worth of all members of the community and special care for the oppressed and the poor. Deuteronomy is not concerned with a casuistic expansion of the law to include every possible juridical issue which might arise; rather, it is concerned with the motivation of the people to do justice in their collective, national life.

Acknowledgment of the deep covenantal ties which bind the people together both in their cultic and also in their secular relationships provides the basis for the establishment of just judicial procedures and structures. In addition to the proclamation of principles and norms, justice also requires the establishment of procedures and a process whereby disputes and hard cases can be equitably resolved as circumstances change (Deut.16:18ff.; 17:8ff.; 19:15ff.). Thus, judges and officers of the various tribes are to render judgments that are "righteous" and "fair." They are forbidden to pervert justice either through partiality or through the taking of bribes. Within these broad guidelines, they are to do that which appears to them to be just (Deut.16:18ff.). Similarly, provision is made for appeal of hard cases to the priests, the Levites, and judges, who are to pass judgment in such matters (Deut.17:8ff.). Clearly, the kinds of judgments which are called for in such circumstances go beyond the letter of particular statutes. What is required is justice patterned ultimately not after the letter of the law but after God's righteousness. The meaning of such justice can never be reduced to ordinances and laws. It must finally be discerned anew in relationship to specific persons in their particular historical settings.

If Old Testament law cannot be equated with the civil law, it is also clear that the two cannot be completely separated. Indeed, there is a certain dialectical relationship between the two. As Eichrodt notes, the covenantal understanding of Israel's relationship to God does not issue in a secularization of the civil law.[21] On the contrary, it implies that the latter is subjected – along with the national life as a whole – to the commandments and the ordinances of the divine covenant. The civil law is part of the ordering process in human history. Determining precisely how the former is to be related to the covenant is an ongoing process which leaves a large measure of freedom to each generation.

According to the Deuteronomist, the covenant which God made with Israel at Horeb was made not with the "fathers," but with the living generation (Deut.5:2–3). Similarly, the commandments and the ordinances are addressed to those who hear them "this day" (Deut.5:1–3; 26:16–19; 29:10–15; 30:1–2,11–16). Both the covenant and the commandments are renewed at the great cultic celebrations where they are recalled and reaffirmed. Thus, the members of each generation stand in the same relation to God as did their forebears at Horeb.[22]

Josiah's bold attempt to reform the nation on the basis of the "book of the law" which had been found in the Temple in Jerusalem (II Kings 21–23) was short-lived.[23] His death in battle (610 BC) was soon followed by the destruction of Jerusalem and the Temple in 586 BC. During the ensuing period of the Exile, the understanding of the law underwent a number of important changes. The law came to occupy a central place in the lives of the Jews in captivity, who were separated both from their home-land and from the Temple. The role of the priests in the preservation and elaboration of the law was greatly expanded. While a number of codes of priestly law occur in the Pentateuch, the best-known of these has come to be called the Holiness Code (Lev.17–26). Much of the legislation included in this collection comes from an earlier period. Here, however, the law has been organized in a different manner in order to reflect the priestly point of view. As the title suggests, this body of law is primarily concerned with preserving the holiness and purity of the people of Israel.

Holiness meant the exclusive worship of God and strict separa-tion from the religious and social practices that were prohibited by Israelite law. The underlying reason for this demand is God's own holiness: "You shall be holy; for I the Lord your God am holy" (Lev.19:2). Significantly, along with the detailed instructions concerning purity, a collection of laws similar to the Decalogue and the Covenant Code is included in Leviticus 19.[24] Here again, just as in Deuteronomy, it is clear that the divine requirement goes far beyond the formal letter of the law and demands an attitude of inward obedience and love. Just as the Deuteronomist summarized all human duties toward God in terms of the single commandment to love God with all of one's heart, soul, and strength, so the Priestly writer summarizes all duties of persons toward each other in terms of the single commandment to love one's neighbor as oneself (Lev.19:18). What the law finally demands is a "readiness to help" one's neighbor, including the poor, the deaf, the blind, the elderly, and strangers, or sojourners.[25] Beyond the formal stipulations of the law, each person is to be treated with respect as a human being. The love commandment applies equally to strangers (resident aliens) and to one's fellow-Israelites: "The stranger who sojourns with you shall be to you as the native [i.e., the homeborn] among you, and you shall love him as yourself; for you were strangers in the land of Egypt: I am the Lord your God" (Lev. 19:34).

Attention has been called to the Holiness Code as an illustration of the kind of legislation that is contained in the Priestly narrative (P) of early Israelite history. Other examples of this kind of law are found throughout the Pentateuch, with the exception of Deuteronomy, which consists largely of the Deuteronomistic legislation (Deut.4:44–30:20) which we have just been considering. Whereas Leviticus is composed entirely of Priestly legislation, however, in Genesis, Exodus, and Numbers such law is embedded in the priestly account of history from its beginning. In the Priestly strand of the Genesis account of creation, God appears as a law-giver at Creation. The divine blessing upon the first man and the first woman is accompanied with a specific command to "be fruitful and multiply," and to replenish and subdue the earth (Gen.1:28). This command applies to all people and not just to Israel. The law prohibiting the taking of human life (Gen.9:5–7) is similarly addressed to humanity as a whole through Noah and his sons.[26]

In the exilic and post-exilic periods, Israel's identity as a people came to be centered increasingly in the law. After their return from captivity in Babylon, the people assembled in a public square in Jerusalem. At their behest, Ezra read to them "the book of the law of Moses," which Nehemiah calls the *"Torah."* Upon hearing that book and its interpretation by the Levites, the people at first wept, but soon their weeping turned to rejoicing as they understood what they had heard. Following the reading of the law, they covenanted together to keep it (Neh.9:38–10:29). While it is uncertain whether the *Torah* which was read on that occasion was the entire Pentateuch or only some portion of the latter, Ezra's promulgation of the law represented a major step in the canonization of the first five books of the Hebrew Scriptures.[27] Canonization itself was a process which extended over several centuries, with roots going back to the pre-exilic period. It had been given increased impetus by Josiah's reformation in the sixth century BC. That reform, it will be recalled, was based upon an early version of Deuteronomy, a copy of which had been found in the Temple.[28] By the time of Ezra, the term, "the book of the law," evidently included the entire Pentateuch; as such these books were collectively called *Torah*. Ezra's ensuing reformation, based upon the Mosaic tradition, marked the end of the period when new law with divine authority could come into being.[29] Through canonization of the *Torah*, Moses came to be revered both as the mediator of the covenant between God and Israel, and as the only authoritative proclaimer of the divinely revealed law.

THE LAW AND THE PROPHETS

There has been much misunderstanding of the relationship of the prophets to law in the Old Testament. It is often assumed that the two stand in polar opposition to each other. Such a misconception is the result of a failure to understand both the law and the prophets in terms of their historical development and, most particularly, in terms of their relationship to the covenant.

As a result of a number of recent studies, it has become clear that the prophets were not isolated individuals, separated either

from the cultic worship or from the teaching of the law.[30] The
moral demands which they made were rooted in the traditions of
law going back to Sinai. The prophets, however, applied these
old ideas in new ways under new conditions. Moreover, the
relationship between the development of pre-exilic law in the Old
Testament and the pre-exilic prophets (Amos, Hosea, Isaiah of
Jerusalem, and Micah) was, in a certain way, dialogical. The
prophets not only borrowed from the existing collections of law;
but also influenced their final formation. (Deuteronomy in its
present form, it is generally agreed, probably comes from the
seventh century BC.)

Just as the law was later re-interpreted as a constitutive part of
the covenant between Yahweh and Israel, so the prophets were
subsequently construed as messengers of Yahweh whose announcements of judgment against Israel were based upon her
unfaithfulness to the covenant. Understood in this way, the
authority both of the law and of the prophets rested ultimately
upon the covenant between Yahweh and Israel, a covenant which
had been instituted at Sinai in the days of Moses.

Although they were familiar with covenants between human
parties, the pre-exilic prophets themselves did not use this image
to describe the unique relationship which existed between
Yahweh and Israel. They spoke, instead, of Israel as Yahweh's
"people" – a people whom he had chosen for his own purposes
and glory.[31] Like the tradition of law, the tradition of Israel as the
people of Yahweh was also deeply rooted in the historical
consciousness of ancient Israel. For example, while the Hebrew
verb *babar* (meaning "to choose, elect" and expressing Yahweh's
special relationship to Israel) first appears in Deuteronomic
literature, the underlying concept itself is very old.[32] It appears in
both the Davidic monarchy tradition associated with Jerusalem
and the Temple and in the Exodus–Sinai tradition associated
with Moses. Both symbolized Yahweh's special grace toward
Israel whom he had chosen to be his people. Subsequently both
came to be known as "election" traditions, and they appear as
such in the present text of the Old Testament. It is this
fundamental idea which is expressed in the covenant. It is also
this fundamental idea of "the people of God" which constituted

the basis for the prophetic demand for justice. More particularly, it constituted the basis not only for their pronouncements of divine judgment upon Israel but also for Israel's ultimate hope of salvation.

In addition to speaking of Israel as the people of God, the prophets also use a variety of other images to express the special quality of this relationship. Amos(3:2) stresses the intimacy which existed between Yahweh and Israel: "You only have I known of all the families of the earth." It is for this reason that she will be punished for all her iniquities. Similarly, Hosea uses the metaphors of husband–wife (Hos.1:2; 2:19) and father–son (Hos.11:1 ff.) to describe the special bond between Yahweh and Israel. In addition to the father–son image (Is.1:2–3; 30:9), Isaiah speaks of Yahweh as the lover and bridegroom, and of Israel as his beloved (Is.5:1). Isaiah also employs the figures of the owner of a vineyard (Is.5:7) and a shepherd and his flock (Is.40:11). On the eve of the Babylonian exile, Jeremiah uses the symbol of a potter shaping clay (Jer.18) as well as the husband–wife metaphor (Jer.3:14; 31:2) for the same purpose. In addition, for the first time among the prophets he also speaks of a covenant between God and Israel. For him, the covenant at Sinai served both as a reminder of the divine commandments (Jer.11:6ff.) and as a guarantee of the divine mercy toward Israel (Jer.14:21). Most strikingly of all, Jeremiah also envisioned a time when God would make a new covenant with Israel and the law would be written upon the hearts of the people (Jer.31:31–33).

The fullest Old Testament expression of God's righteousness and, consequently, of his demand for justice, is found in the sixth-to-eighth-century prophets. Three terms which are used in this context are particularly important: justice (*mishpat*), righteousness (*tsedeq*), and love/mercy (*hesed*). While each of these concepts has its own distinctive usage, in the end, all three must be understood together. In the process of their interaction, each becomes transformed by their common relationship to God.[33]

The prophets are unanimous in declaring that Yahweh requires justice (*mishpat*) on the part of those who worship him and that the standard of human conduct is the divine righteousness (*tsedeq*).[34] In its original usage, *mishpat* meant the judgment which was given by a judge; hence, it might also mean justice, ordinance, legal right, or law. In the Old Testament the concept came to be equated with God's law and the divine justice. *Mishpat* frequently meant judgments that were based upon precedent, but the precedent was itself understood as the word of God. Beyond justice (*mishpat*), however, the righteousness (*tsedeq*) of Yahweh also includes mercy (*hesed*). *Hesed* refers fundamentally to an enduring relationship of love, kindness, or faithfulness. It is rendered variously into English as "steadfast love" (Hos.2:19,6:6), "faithfulness" (Jer.31:3), and "loving kindness" (Hos.2:19; Jer.31:3, ASV). It is also sometimes translated as "mercy" (cf. Jer.3:12: "for I am merciful, says the Lord"). To know God is to know that he is "the Lord who does kindness, justice, and righteousness in the earth" (Jer.9:23–24).[35] These are the things in which he "delights," and these are what he demands of his people.

For the prophets, God's righteousness is manifest not only in the judgments which he metes out in human history but even more in his acts of mercy and salvation toward Israel and, ultimately, toward all peoples. God's righteousness transcends his justice. The former does not negate the latter, however; rather, in the divine righteousness strict, or legal, justice is transformed by love/mercy and thus becomes redemptive.

Although the pre-exilic prophets are sometimes referred to as "the ethical prophets of the eighth century," they were first of all religious prophets. "Their insistence upon right-conduct," Snaith writes, "was religious in its origin, and at root was never anything else than religious."[36] They felt themselves called and commissioned by God to be his spokesmen. When Amaziah, the priest of Bethel, admonishes Amos to go back to Judah and prophesy there, Amos tells him forthrightly why he must speak out at Bethel: "The Lord took me from following the flock, and the Lord said to me, 'Go, prophesy to my people Israel.' Now therefore hear the word of the Lord" (Amos 7:15,16). For Jeremiah, the word of the Lord is as "a burning fire shut up in my bones" (Jer.20:9). Similarly, the Lord tells Isaiah: "Go forth to meet Ahaz ... at the end of the conduit of the upper pool on the highway to the Fuller's field, and say to him ..." (Is.7:3).

Since Yahweh is sovereign over all the nations, his demand for justice is universal. Not only is he guardian of Israelite law but also of the entire moral order, including the conventional norms of international behavior. The charges which the prophets make both against individuals and against nations are specific and particular.[37] Lists of oracles against the nations are found in Amos 1–2, Is.13–23, and Jer.46–51. A similar list is also found in Ezekiel 25–32, dating from the period of the Babylonian Exile. Jeremiah was appointed "a prophet to the nations" even before his birth (Jer.1:5). In Isaiah, Jeremiah, and Ezekiel, the nations and foreign cities are especially condemned for their pride in exalting themselves above God. Damascus and the Ammonites will be punished for their atrocities in warfare (Amos 1:3–5,13–15). Gaza will be destroyed because she has carried a whole people into exile (Amos 1:6–8). Tyre is similarly condemned for engagement in slave trade (Amos 1:9), and Moab for the desecration of the dead (Amos 2:1–3). Most shockingly of all, Amos announces that Judah and Israel will also be punished for their transgressions. Judah has forsaken the law and statutes of Yahweh (Amos 2:4–5). Israel likewise stands condemned "because [the people] sell the righteous for silver, and the needy for a pair of shoes – they ... trample the head of the poor into the dust of the earth, and turn aside the way of the afflicted" (Amos 2:6,7). The accusations of Hosea and Micah are similar. In Israel "there is swearing, lying, killing, stealing, and committing adultery; they break all bounds and murder follows murder" (Hos.4:2). The merchants use rigged balances and deceitful weights (Mic.6:11; cf. Amos 8:5).

Yahweh's demand for justice cannot be appeased by sacrifices, peace offerings, and ceremonial forms of religion (Amos 5:21–24; Mic.3:9–12). Oppression of the poor and needy is strongly condemned (Amos 8:4–6; cf.Mic.6:1ff.); and special concern is expressed for widows and orphans. This does not mean that there is one standard of morality for the rich and another for the poor. On the contrary, there is a single standard for all; but since in common practice the needy and the poor do not receive equal treatment with the rich, they are singled out for special concern because their need is particularly great. Justice means the restoration of a condition of normalcy in society, a return to a condition of equity which had once prevailed before the social order itself became disrupted by greed and oppression.[38] Justice means, for example, the restoration of small land holdings which had been appropriated from the peasants by the owners of large estates (Is.3:14,15). It means restitution to the poor for injustices in the marketplace (Amos 8:4–6). Since the judges themselves are corrupt, the poor and the oppressed do not have any redress in the courts; hence, the community itself is obligated to champion their cause. Amos' appeal is addressed to Israel as a whole: "... let justice roll down like waters, and righteousness like an ever-flowing stream" (Amos 5:24). So it is also with Micah's dramatic account of God's controversy with his people. In response to Israel's query concerning the kind of worship which is pleasing to God, Micah replies that Yahweh requires three things, namely, "to do justice, to love kindness, and to walk humbly with your God" (Mic.6:8).

The Hebrew word which the prophets characteristically use for "sin" is *pesha*. Although this term also means "rebellion," it is frequently rendered into English as "transgression." By itself, however, this translation is misleading, for it suggests that the prophets' view of sin is essentially the transgression of moral law. Thus, it fails to capture the personal quality of Israel's relationship with Yahweh. "Rebellion," on the other hand, means an active turning away from God's sovereign will. For the prophets *sin* is fundamentally a religious term. It includes acts of transgression, but it also refers to a broken relationship between God and humanity. Amos' accusations are stated primarily in terms of acts of disobedience, which have resulted in Israel's estrangement from God. "Repentance" means "returning" to the Lord (Amos 4:6,8–11). It signifies "seeking" God that Israel might live (Amos 5:4). It entails "establishing justice in the gate"; at a deeper level, it also denotes "hating evil and loving good" (Amos 5:15).

Amos' denunciations are focused primarily upon acts of transgression. In contrast, Hosea turns, first of all, to the inner, personal relationship which has been broken. The fundamental controversy which God has with Israel is that there is "no faithfulness, or kindness, and no knowledge of God in the land" (Hos.4:1). Israel has played the harlot and worshipped other gods

(Hos.1:2; 3:1). Ephraim, also, has "dealt faithlessly" with God and "rebelled" against him (Hos.6:7; 7:13). Isaiah opens his prophecy against Israel by recalling the intimacy of the relationship between Yahweh and his people: "Sons have I reared and brought-up," says the Lord, "but they have rebelled against me" (Is.1:2; cf.30:1,9). As a consequence of her rebellion, Israel has become a "sinful nation," a people who are "utterly estranged" from God (Is.1:4). Jeremiah similarly accuses Israel not only of having rebelled against God (Jer.4:17) but, more fundamentally still, of having "a stubborn and rebellious heart" (Jer.5:23). For Hosea, Isaiah, and Jeremiah sin is a radical perversion of the heart and will. While it is expressed in acts of transgression, it refers fundamentally to a relationship between God and humanity which has been broken by unfaithfulness, disloyalty, and pride.[39]

If the prophets see God's fundamental requirement as justice, and judgment as his punishment for injustice, they nevertheless see his steadfast love as ultimately transcending his wrath. The word of judgment is not canceled, but neither is it God's final word. Israel has been like an unfaithful bride and deserves only punishment, but Yahweh promises to restore her unto himself because of his love for her: "I will betroth you to me forever; I will betroth you to me in righteousness (*tsedeq*) and in justice (*mishpat*), in steadfast love (*hesed*), and in mercy. I will betroth you to me in faithfullness ..." (Hos.2:19–20). Even Amos, who is perhaps the most relentless of all the prophets in his insistence upon the divine judgment, holds out the hope that Yahweh may yet be gracious to a remnant of Joseph if this remnant will turn away from evil and seek good (Amos 5:14–15). Jeremiah foretells a new covenant which Yahweh will make with the house of Israel. It will be written upon the hearts of the people; and "they shall all know me, from the least of them to the greatest ... for I will forgive their iniquity, and I will remember their sin no more" (Jer.31:31–34). However, it is Isaiah of the Exile who most clearly sees God acting redemptively in order to save his people for his own sake: "For my name's sake I defer my anger, for the sake of my praise I restrain it for you, that I may not cut you off" (Is.48:9). The servant of the Lord will suffer vicariously for the wicked, and as the result of his chastisement many will be accounted righteous and healed (Is.53:5,11). Israel has been chosen, not for special privilege, but "as a light to the nations, that my salvation may reach to the end of the earth" (Is.49:6). A new and eternal covenant based upon the divine mercy will be instituted, and salvation will be freely offered to all peoples: "Turn to me and be saved, all the ends of the earth! For I am God, and there is no other .... To me every knee shall bow, every tongue shall swear" (Is.45:22–23; cf.55:3; 56:6–8).

THE STRUCTURE OF COVENANTAL JUSTICE

The covenant which Yahweh made with Israel at Sinai provides the basic structure of Israel's self-understanding as the people of God. While the concept of such a covenant represents a much later development in Hebrew thought, it was subsequently used by the Deuteronomic editors of the Pentateuch to interpret the history of Yahweh's relationship to Israel from its beginning onward. Not only does the Exodus–Sinai narrative express the dramatic involvement of God in human history; it also symbolizes the moral nature of God's relationship to the world.

The covenant at Sinai is mutually binding; it is based upon reciprocal obligations between Yahweh and Israel. It includes a collection of commandments, together with the promise of blessings and curses. The people accept the covenant and pledge their obedience. Viewed from this perspective, Israel's subsequent history is a story of her unfaithfulness to the covenant and God's faithfulness to his people, which extends beyond judgment to forgiveness and reconciliation.

Covenantal justice is, first of all, *theocentric*. God's righteousness is the standard by which all human justice is finally measured. It is revealed in the commandments; it is also made known through the creating, ordering, and reconciling action of God in history. Justice is not simply a principle or an ideal. It is a reality which is coming to pass. Justice is the manifestation of God's sovereignty in the moral order which he has established. "In the eyes of the prophets," writes Heschel, "justice is charged with the omnipotence of God. What ought to be, shall be."[40] The biblical notion of eschatology expresses the same confidence in the ultimate triumph of righteousness, for God himself will bring it to pass. The prophets' announcements of impending judgment and the coming day of salvation are based upon their perceptions of what God is doing in and through the events of human history.

Secondly, covenantal justice is *relational* rather than abstract. It is primarily concerned with meeting the needs of the neighbor rather than with the conformity of human action to ideal patterns of the good or obedience to absolute moral laws. Justice means faithfulness to the neighbor. Understood in covenantal terms, justice includes the rights of socially marginalized groups; it also includes the obligation of the community to redress the injustices which such groups have received and to treat them with fairness and equality. While the needs of the poor and the oppressed have provided the basis for individual rights claims in modern liberal societies, in Israelite culture the relationship between individuals and the community was interdependent. Justice was not only a rights claim arising out of the needs of the disadvantaged; from a covenantal perspective, it was a communal obligation grounded in Israel's vocation to be God's people. Justice was a demand for faithfulness in the life of the community as a whole, a demand which rested ultimately not upon human rights but upon Israel's covenantal relationship to God.

Thirdly, covenantal justice is fundamentally *equalitarian* and *inclusive* in its estimate of human worth. The claims of justice are grounded finally in the common humanity which all persons share in their relationship to God. Although the promise of equality remained unfulfilled in Israel, it nevertheless constitutes a basic standard in terms of which all human systems of justice are finally measured. Covenantal justice is biased towards the weak, the needy, and the oppressed. Their claims to justice are especially great on account of their vulnerability and lack of power. For this reason God hears their cry and champions their cause. Though slavery remained an accepted institution, slaves were protected from maiming (Ex.21:26–27). Hebrew slaves were to be set free each fiftieth year (Lev.25:10). To prevent exploitation of the poor, the land also was to be redistributed in the year of jubilee (Lev.25:23–28). Justice meant showing hospitality to strangers and resident aliens, for the Israelites, too, were once strangers and sojourners in the land of Egypt.

FORMS OF JUSTICE

The Hebrew concept of justice is concrete and particular. Just as God's righteousness is manifest in his specific historical acts of election, deliverance, judgment, and salvation, so human justice is expressed concretely in the historical, collective life of Israel as the people of God.

In classical Greek thought, the final norm of justice is defined in terms of an ideal good, namely, the common good. In Hebraic thought, it is defined in terms of divinely given commandments. While the Mosaic covenant includes both categorical (apodictic) and case (casuistic, procedural) law, the former most clearly expresses the distinctiveness of Israelite law. Every collection of normative materials in the Old Testament contains similar categorical demands.[41] These are typically stated in the form of commands or exhortations, and they are usually expressed as the words of Deity. In addition to the Ten Commandments, other examples include the following: "You shall not wrong a stranger or oppress him, for you were strangers in the land of Egypt. You shall not afflict any widow or orphan" (Ex. 22:21–22). "You shall do no wrong in judgment, in measures of length or weight or quantity. You shall have just balances, just weights, a just ephah (a dry measure), and a just hin (a liquid measure)" (Lev.19:35). "Cursed be he who dishonors his father or his mother ... Cursed be he who perverts the justice due to the sojourner, the fatherless, and the widow" (Deut.27:16–19).

While both forms of law – apodictic and casuistic – were included in the legal traditions of Israel, neither constituted state law. Casuistic law, exemplified by the ordinances in the Book of the Covenant (Ex.20:22–23:33), represented an attempt to adapt and apply the commandments to various cases which might arise and to establish penalties for the violation of such statutes and ordinances. The commandments, on the other hand, formed the distinctive ethico-religious core of Israelite *Torah*. In order to distinguish the commandments from state law – and also from case law – the former are perhaps best understood as "rules of righteousness."[42] They established the basis for a powerful critique of conventional law, including both Israelite case law and civil law. They were the normative center of an ongoing internal dialogue within Israel concerning the relationship between the covenant and conventional, or customary, law and morality. As participants in this dialogue, the prophets criticized the latter in terms of the commandments. Thus they prepared the way both for the revision of traditional case law and for a deeper understanding of the covenant.

The injustices which the prophets denounced – the extraction of taxes and fines, enforcement of creditors' rights, foreclosures, and commitment of persons to bond servitude and slavery – were "legal" in the sense that they were sanctioned by conventional – or positive – law. The harshest indictments of the prophets were directed against the rich and the powerful who used the legal system, particularly the courts, to pervert justice. Those in positions of power "trample upon the poor"; they take bribes and "turn aside the needy in the gate" (Amos.5:11,12). "Woe to those who decree iniquitous decrees, and the writers who keep writing oppression, to turn aside the needy from justice and to rob the poor ... of their right" (Is.10:1–2). Speaking of the officials in Jerusalem, Isaiah declares: "Everyone loves a bribe and runs after gifts. They do not defend the orphan, and the widow's case is not heard" (Is.1:21–26).[43] Against all such laws and procedures the prophets insisted that justice is both the foundation and the ultimate criterion of all law. Moreover, the final measure of all true justice is found in the justice and righteousness of God.

This religious tradition of God's justice and righteousness is everywhere presupposed by the prophets. Yahweh's special relationship to Israel, the divinely given commandments together with the promised blessings and curses, and the specification of particular forms of injustice, are all included in the biblical story of God's action in human history. The prophets do not proclaim new moral standards. Rather, they call upon Israel to remember her special vocation as God's people, to obey the commandments, and, particularly, to do justice and righteousness, which are God's primary demands. Israel will be judged by these standards.

Because of her transgressions, the day of the Lord will be "darkness, and not light" (Amos 5:18). The Lord "looked for justice [and] righteousness," Isaiah declares, but found, instead, that the weak were oppressed, the guilty were acquitted for a bribe, and the innocent deprived of their rights (Is.5:7,23). Israel has "rejected the law of the Lord"; therefore, she will be punished (Is.5:24). But since God's righteousness includes mercy, beyond the coming day of judgment the prophets also proclaim a time of deliverance and salvation not only of Israel but, through Israel, of all peoples.

In addition to outward acts of obedience, justice also requires an inner disposition – a readiness – to keep the commandments out of a sense of gratitude, praise, and affection. It includes not only just deeds but also a quality of character. A just person is one who "delights in" justice and is, for this reason, inclined to do justice. A just person possesses the qualities of mercy, compassion, faithfulness, and love. These virtues are prerequisite for the keeping of the commandments; they are also essential qualities of judges in the application of law to individual cases. To fulfill the commandments is to love God with all one's heart, soul, and strength (Deut.6:15); it is also to love one's neighbor as oneself (Lev.19:18).

Covenantal justice is, finally, reconciling justice. Tillich calls this "transforming" or "creative" justice.[44] In contrast, Aristotelian justice is fundamentally preserving justice, which seeks to sustain the existing social order. If a disruption of that order occurs, justice means the restoration of society to its previous state. Preserving justice means rendering to each person his or her "due" based upon conventional criteria of personal ability, merit, rank, or wealth. If the established order is unjust, systemic injustice continues. If people were unequal before their customary roles and relationships were broken, then they remain so when such relationships are restored. The poor are still poor; the oppressed, still oppressed; and the marginalized remain marginal.[45]

In contrast to preserving justice, reconciling justice seeks the transformation of all forms of human society and culture. From a biblical perspective, all historical systems of justice are corrupted and perverted by sin; therefore, they fall ultimately under judgment by the righteousness and justice of God. Covenantal justice demands the transformation of hierarchal forms of society upon the basis of the fundamental equality and liberty which all share through their creation in the "image of God." Reconciling justice means equal justice. It means sharing of power with those who are oppressed. It means participation of marginalized groups in institutionalized forms of economic and political power. Reconciling justice demands the resignation of proportionate (retributive and distributive) justice out of compassion for the needy and for the sake of the well-being of the community as a whole. Creative justice forgives in order that broken relationships may be restored. "Justice in its ultimate meaning is creative justice, and creative justice is the form of reuniting love" – that is, "the form in which and through which love performs its work."[46]

Although Israel remained hierarchical in its social structure, belief in the basic equality and liberty of all persons remained an essential part of the covenantal heritage. As part of that tradition, these ideas have continued to constitute basic norms whereby contemporary forms of oppression and injustice are challenged and criticized in light of new experiences of freedom and equality under changing historical conditions. In the following chapter we turn to Puritanism in England and America for a paradigmatic attempt to build the foundation of community and justice upon the biblical ideas of covenant and the righteousness of God.

CHAPTER 4

Justice in the Puritan covenantal tradition

Covenant theology, as it developed in England and America in the sixteenth and seventeenth centuries, represented an attempt to restate the traditional Calvinist doctrines of divine sovereignty, grace and works, and religious and civil authority in light of the growth and spread of new ideas of human freedom, autonomy, and individual rights associated with the Renaissance and Enlightenment. These ideas were also associated with contractualist theories of the state which had arisen during the Renaissance and subsequently spread throughout Western Europe.

HISTORICAL BACKGROUND

Although Puritan Covenantal thought drew both upon indigenous English notions of covenant and upon the rich heritage of medieval moral theology, its theological roots are found primarily in the Reformed branch of the Protestant Reformation.[1] John Calvin (1509–1564) provided the most systematic and influential statement of Reformed theology in his famous *Institutes of the Christian Religion*. Despite his influence upon Puritanism, however, Calvin was not a covenant theologian. His impact upon Puritanism was due, rather, to the force of his theology as a whole. His teaching was based upon the doctrine of divine sovereignty with a strong emphasis upon election and predestination. For him, covenant was an unconditional promise of salvation to the elect. Good works were, therefore, a sign of election, not a condition of it.

Calvin also influenced the course of Puritanism in England and Scotland through his doctrine of the duty of lesser magistrates to resist tyrants.[2] The duty of resistance, he argued, is grounded in the obligation of rulers to protect the liberty of the people. Such resistance is a matter of conscience, undertaken in obedience to God. It is a duty that pertains to the office of lower rulers who also have a responsibility for the divinely appointed ordinance of governance. Private individuals are not permitted to resist the ruling authorities; on the contrary, they are commanded only to obey. The Calvinist doctrine of resistance exercised a profound influence upon Puritan leaders such as John Knox in Scotland and Oliver Cromwell in England. Not only did it provide justification for political revolution; it also provided powerful motivation for it through the concept of the vocation of the elect.

In addition to Calvin, Puritanism in England was also influenced by Zwingli (1484–1531) and his associates in Zurich and the surrounding region of the Rhine. Here the Evangelical movement was rooted in a cultural tradition of humanism, local self-government, and a contract theory of the state grounded in natural law.[3] In a commentary on Isaiah, written in 1525, Oecolampadius interpreted the divine covenant with humanity in terms of a contract. Attainment of the blessing contained in the covenant was made contingent upon humanity's obedience to the law of love. This law was written upon the human heart at Creation; subsequently its meaning has been more clearly revealed in the written law of the Bible. Drawing upon the late medieval notion of a state contract, the Rhineland reformers also developed the theory of a contract between rulers and subjects based upon natural law. This idea was used to limit the authority of kings.

As a result of the persecution during the reign of the Catholic Queen Mary I (1553–1558), many Protestant refugees from England fled to the continent. Some settled in Geneva, where they came under the influence of Calvin. Others settled in Zurich and the Rhineland, where they were introduced to the contract notion of the covenant. Upon their return from the continent, the exiles in the vicinity of Zurich incorporated this idea into their own teaching about the covenant. Both in Zurich and in Geneva the refugees gained a new understanding of the authority of

Scripture in matters of worship, ecclesiastical polity, and civil governance. These beliefs were common elements in Reformed Protestantism; as such they became essential features of covenantal thought both in England and in New England.

Covenant theology – or federal theology as it was commonly called in New England – came to its fullest expression in America in the middle of the seventeenth century. In the end, however, covenant and contract proved to be an unstable alliance. As a particular form of theology, federal theology soon passed from the scene. This does not mean, however, that it was a failure. Its role was mediational.[4] It represents a major attempt to restate the profoundly biblical notion of covenant in a new set of historical circumstances. As such it constitutes an important legacy for the self-understanding not only of individuals but also of a people.[5]

The importance of this legacy is attested by the attention which it has received from scholars in a number of different fields since the publication of *The New England Mind* by Perry Miller in 1939. Many of these analyses have tended, however, either to ignore the essential theological grounding of this movement in Calvin and in English Evangelicalism, or to exaggerate the individualistic character of Puritan ethics through failure to give adequate attention to such communal themes as religious and civil covenants, equity, virtue, and the common good.

Thus Perry Miller, for example, interpreted covenantal theology as an attempt to resolve the antinomy in Calvinist doctrine between determinism and human freedom by making salvation dependent upon good works. While the idea of such a conditional covenant was fundamentally inconsistent with the traditional Calvinist doctrine of decrees, Miller argued, it nevertheless provided a pragmatic (albeit unstable) means of reconciling human freedom and moral responsibility with the doctrine of decrees. When one examines such early covenantal writers as Perkins, Preston, Sibbes, and Ames, however, one finds that they turned to the imagery of covenant primarily out of the need to provide a basis for assurance of salvation and moral guidance, not to resolve a conflict between predestination and human freedom. Not only did Miller's focus upon the problem of decrees cause

him to misconstrue the relationship between Calvin and covenantal thought in important respects; it also caused him to neglect
the evangelical sources of covenantal theology and ethics.[6]

In contrast to Miller, Michael Walzer describes Puritanism in
England in the period 1530–1660 as an "ideology of social
transition." The Puritanism of this period was, he believes,
essentially a product of Calvinism, which influenced England
primarily through the refugees who settled in Geneva during the
Marian Exile. They went beyond Calvin's teaching on resistance
by lesser magistrates and developed a doctrine of resistance and
revolution by the elect against unjust rulers.[7]

Puritanism provided a way of dealing with the breakdown of
the older English society – its hierarchical structure, its patriarchal
character, and its organic conception of society – that resulted
from deep-rooted processes of social change. In its early stages
Puritanism contributed to this social disintegration, but subsequently it provided a way of restructuring society based upon the
divine sovereignty, the vocation of the saints, and the idea of a
holy commonwealth.

Due to its deep consciousness of sin, Puritanism was basically
repressive and sought to impose discipline and restraint upon
society, whereas Locke and liberal thinkers relied much more
strongly upon the goodness of human nature, upon virtue, and
upon voluntary self-control to achieve the welfare of the community as a whole. But despite its authoritarian and repressive
stance, Puritanism indirectly helped prepare the way for the
acceptance of liberal and democratic ideas in a new social
setting.[8] This influence was mediated in large part through the
Puritan doctrines of the covenantal basis of social institutions,
government by consent, and constitutional limitations on government as well as by their congregational polity. In much the same
way, Walzer believes, Puritanism also contributed to the growth
of capitalism through the moral discipline which it encouraged.
Instead of encouraging acquisitiveness, however, Puritanism
sought to combat and control it.[9]

Before turning to the covenant writers themselves, it will be
helpful to examine briefly another recent study of English
Puritanism which brings the issue of individualism into sharper

focus. Like Walzer, David Zaret also views Puritan covenant theology as an instrument of social control. Unlike Walzer, however, Zaret interprets the former as a means of clerical control over the elect rather than as an ideology of repression by the elect, both clerical and lay. Thus understood, covenant theology was a response of the clergy to a variety of lay movements of dissent and protest which threatened to undermine the leadership and control of the clergy in religious affairs.

Many social and cultural developments contributed to a more active role for the laity. The revolution in printing resulted in a far wider circulation of books and pamphlets, including the Bible, and there was an accompanying growth of popular literary culture. Also religious beliefs and forms of worship were increasingly rationalized in the sixteenth century, and market forms of economy were spreading not only in the cities and towns but throughout the English countryside.[10] The increased availability of the Bible together with the dissemination of popular religious tracts resulted in disputes about the authority and interpretation of Scripture, the place of liturgy and the Mass in worship, and the role and authority of the clergy. Debates over such matters posed threats both to religious orthodoxy and to the authority of the clergy. Frequently, such disputes were associated with strong anticlerical sentiments.

In order to make Calvinism more palatable to the laity and thus maintain control over them, the Puritan clerics reinterpreted the traditional Calvinist doctrine in the form of covenant theology. The centerpiece of this theology was the idea of a "heavenly contract," patterned after the familiar form of economic contracts.[11] Through the adoption of this idea the clerics sought to create a balance between the demands of their own institutional roles, and the new self-perception and independence of the laity. Most importantly, they interpreted the covenant as a contract and used the terms interchangeably. In the ensuing redefinition of roles, the clergy assumed responsibility for proclaiming the terms of "the heavenly contract" while satisfaction of these terms rested with individual believers.

Zaret does not argue that covenant theology was the product of economic determinism. Instead, his thesis is that the widespread use of market contracts constituted a major source of this theological development and that the contract idea was fundamentally individualistic. While his conception of the relationship between philosophical and economic forces is interactive rather than reductionist, in the end the market model of contract determines the meaning of covenant. This is true, he contends, both regarding God's relationship to humanity and regarding the standards for measuring equity, truth, and justice.[12]

Zaret seriously overstates the individualism and distorts the impact of covenant theology as a whole. In a sense he acknowledges this point when he concedes: "of course the social implications of a market rationality and of possessive individualism ... would not have met with Puritan approval. *Amoral individualism in economic and political life was anathema to Puritanism*" [my italics].[13] Not only was such individualism anathema to the Puritans; they themselves made this point plain in their warnings against avarice and in their teachings about the primacy of the public good over individual interest.

It is not clear from Zaret's analysis why Puritans would consider anathema an idea which they exalted to the status of "the heavenly contract," thus making it the very "marrow of Puritan divinity."[14] Thus, the question which Zaret's analysis poses for our study is twofold. In the first place, is the idea of covenant in Puritanism as contractarian and as individualistic as he implies? Secondly, are any countervailing forces provided by other features of covenant theology? Do not strictures against avarice and admonitions to seek the public good provide limits to acquisitive individualism? Stated in more positive terms, does not the Calvinist doctrine of vocation provide the basis for precisely such limits?

Attention to the concept of justice in the covenantal writers themselves provides a much-needed corrective to the foregoing analyses of Puritanism. Such a study discloses important continuities between Calvin and Puritanism regarding reason and revelation, works and grace, and the forms and criteria of justice. At the same time it makes clear the inadequacy of any attempt to reduce covenantal theology either to an instrument of social control or to an expression of unrestrained individualism. In addition, analysis of covenantal justice also reveals its broader foundation not only in Calvinism but also in medieval moral theology.

THE TWO COVENANTS: WORKS AND GRACE [15]

At the heart of covenant theology was the doctrine of two covenants between God and humanity, one based on works and the other on grace. For Calvin there was only one covenant, namely a covenant of grace. This included both God's covenant with Israel and the covenant which was established through Christ. In terms of their substance these two covenants are "the very same."[16] The differences between them are differences only in administration. Calvin's concern at this point was to clarify the relationship between the Old and the New Testaments and, more particularly, the relationship between law and gospel. In sharp contrast to those who maintained that in the Old Testament salvation is based upon law whereas in the New Testament it is based upon grace, Calvin insisted that from the beginning salvation has always rested upon grace and that all of those whom God has called are subject to the same law. The covenant by which the patriarchs, the lawgivers, and the prophets were united to God was founded, not on any merits of their own, but exclusively upon the divine mercy.

In order to clarify the relationship between faith and works in the Calvinist doctrine of grace, the covenant theologians added the idea of a prior covenant between God and Adam based upon works.[17] In this agreement God promised to reward Adam and his posterity with eternal life if Adam fulfilled certain obligations. These duties were stipulated in the moral law. Moreover, this law was implanted in Adam's heart at Creation so that obedience would be natural and intuitive. The original covenant of works was thus based upon the law of nature. Had Adam remained obedient, he and his descendants would have known this law by nature, and they would have ordered their lives by it. Because he failed to keep the covenant, however, Adam fell. As a result of the Fall, human nature became corrupted, so that not only Adam but also his posterity were deserving of punishment. But God, in his mercy, entered into a new covenant with humankind, beginning with Abraham.[18]

Like the covenant with Adam, that with Abraham was also an agreement containing the mutual obligations of both parties. God promised salvation to the patriarch and his descendants; Abraham, for his part, was required to believe God's promise. Since fallen humanity is unable to initiate faith, God freely bestows saving grace upon the elect. Such grace is the efficient cause of faith. Apart from grace, humanity is unable either to believe or to obey the law. The covenant of grace which God initiated with Abraham continues into the Christian era. Although the covenant of grace is distinguished into two testaments, they are one in substance.[19] In both instances salvation depends solely upon faith. For Abraham, however, faith was belief in the promise of salvation; it was belief in the Christ who was yet to come. For Christians, on the other hand, faith is belief that this promise has already been fulfilled.

Just as Calvin had taught that the moral law of the Old Testament remained binding after the coming of Christ, so the federal theologians held that the commandments contained in the covenant of works also remained binding since they, too, had been restated in the Decalogue. Yet the moral law disclosed in the Old Testament and the moral law which was presupposed in the covenant of works were not precisely the same. For Perkins, the Decalogue is an abridgement of the whole law and the covenant of works.[20] According to Preston, the covenant of works was originally made with Adam, and it was restated by Moses in terms of the moral law.[21] Similarly, Sibbes declared that the covenant of works had been first made with Adam in paradise and that it had been "renewed in the delivery of the ten commandments."[22] According to Ames, all of the precepts of the moral law save that concerning the sabbath are based on the law of nature.[23] In general, in its Adamic form the covenant of works rested fundamentally upon the law of nature, which was knowable through reason and natural inclination, whereas the moral law contained in the Old Testament (the Ten Commandments) was disclosed through revelation. The possibility of appeal to natural law had far-reaching implications for the moral foundations of civil law and for the justification and critique of social institutions.[24] On the one hand, natural law presupposes the capacity to discern the basic precepts of the moral law through reason; yet on the other hand, the moral law which is discerned by reason can never be fully equated with God's righteousness as the final norm of justice. Although the natural law can be perceived only dimly apart from revelation, it nevertheless points to a transcendent moral order by which all institutions and positive law are finally measured. Since the Fall, only certain "relics" of the law of nature remain in the hearts of all people. Such imprints are indispensable, however, for they provide an essential basis for human community. For Puritans such as Ames and Baxter, as well as Ames' followers in America, God orders human history both through the law of nature and through the divine law revealed in Scripture.

THE COVENANTAL BASIS OF COMMUNITY

The covenant of grace and the covenant of works were thus inseparably woven together in federal theology. The covenant of works was incorporated into the covenant of grace "not as the condition of salvation but as the rule of righteousness."[25] Covenant constituted the basis and the form not only of humanity's relationships with God but also of all ecclesiastical and civil relationships as well. The idea was both individualistic and communal. The covenant of grace was, in the first instance, God's promise of blessing to individuals whom he had elected. This promise was voluntarily assented to by individual believers, along with the obligation to fulfill certain duties to God and also to one another. Such duties were both individual and collective. Just as the promise of grace which had been given to Abraham was addressed through him to Israel, so the covenant of grace made known in Christ is addressed not only to each member of the elect, but also to the community of believers as a whole. Thus the covenant of grace which is initiated with individuals is at the same time a covenant with the people of God collectively.

The collective implications of the covenant are seen most clearly in the idea of a national covenant based upon the paradigm of Israel. For Perkins such an idea was implicit in the doctrine of a double covenant.[26] Like Israel, England had been richly blessed, both spiritually and materially; yet she had proven even more ungrateful and disobedient than the Israelites. She had broken her covenant with God and deserved punishment. Perkins proceeded to enumerate the "common sins of England": ignorance of God's will and worship, contempt of the Christian religion, blasphemy, profanation of the sabbath, and injustice.[27] Unless the people, – that is, all of the people – repented, they would reap the divine judgment.

As Michael McGiffert has ably documented, Perkins called upon the people themselves to assume responsibility for national reform through repentance and renewed individual obedience. In place of the earlier elitist strategy of reform through acts of the queen or parliament, Perkins and his followers sought to "moralize" the nation on the basis of an appeal to the national covenant between God and the people.[28] "By freeing covenant from politics and re-orienting it toward morality," McGiffert writes, "Perkins signalled the way by which Puritanism, having lost a party, might gain a nation."[29] Similarly, Walzer suggests that Perkins represented the beginning of a long process whereby the Puritan clergy "began to educate a national public" through the medium of the sermon.[30] For Perkins and the author of *The Reformation of Religion by Josiah*, the national covenant constituted a basis for exhorting the entire populace – not just the elect – to repentance and the work of national reformation.

The idea of a national covenant was given political expression both in Scotland and in England during the seventeenth century. Thus, the National Covenant of Scotland (1638) issued in the establishment of Presbyterianism. Through the enactment of this covenant, church polity and worship were reformed; the people were bound together to defend the national church against all errors and corruptions; and they were also bound by oath to defend the liberties and laws of the land against all their enemies.[31] In England also there were efforts to bring about national reform through the establishment of Puritanism. The most dramatic and successful of these attempts was the revolt led by Cromwell against Charles I. While the resulting rule of the saints was, as Walzer reminds us, short-lived, the revolution which the Puritans envisaged was a transformation of England into a holy commonwealth through a renewal of the national covenant. Richard Baxter, for example, defended his participation in the struggle of Parliament against the King on the ground that he had violated the rights and liberties which the people had reserved to themselves in their contract with him.[32] For Baxter, the contract between subjects and their rulers rested upon a more fundamental covenant between the people and God, namely, that as a people they would be ruled according to the law of God.

In federal theology all forms of community which do not rest upon conquest or natural relationships such as parent-and-child are based upon contract or covenant. These terms were frequently used interchangeably to signify the nature of voluntary associations as being based upon mutual agreement or consent. All such relationships are essentially triadic. God is always the primary party, and human accountability is finally understood in terms of accountability to God. Thus, while the people are free to enter into a covenant with magistrates to establish a commonwealth, the magistrates are bound by the moral law rather than the will of their subjects. For the Puritans, true civil liberty meant consent to be governed in accordance with God's law through the administration of magistrates. In the words of John Winthrop, it was " a liberty to that only which is good, just and honest."[33]

The Puritan writers were primarily concerned with two major forms of human covenant, namely, the civil and the ecclesiastical. Just as people become citizens of civil societies by entering into voluntary agreements and covenants, so also do they become members of the church by solemn covenant.[34] "For as all citizens are admitted into *jus Civitatis*, and become free Denizens, by voluntarily entering into the common agreement and covenant, whereby they become a Political-body," Davenport declared, "so it is in the Church."[35] In both instances the members of the respective bodies determine the particular form of government which is to be established and the limits of power to be set both for magistrates and for officers in the church. Like the Puritans generally, John Cotton believed that temporal power resides fundamentally in the people. He also believed that rulers are universally inclined towards tyranny. Hence it is necessary, he declared, to ensure that "all power that is on earth be limited, church-power or other."[36] Thomas Hooker, founder of Hartford, expressed a similar view in his Election Sermon of 1638. The choice of public magistrates belongs to the people, he proclaimed.[37] They have the power to set limitations on rulers, for the authority which the latter exercise rests ultimately in "the free consent of the people."

The Puritan covenantal ideal was given classic expression by John Winthrop in a lay sermon entitled, "A Model of Christian Charity," delivered en route to New England in 1630. Winthrop spoke of both the religious and the civil forms of government which he and his companions were commissioned by Divine Providence to establish in Massachusetts. The work which they had in hand, he declared, was "by mutual consent, through a special overruling Providence and a more than ordinary approbation of the churches of Christ to seek out a place of cohabitation and consortship, under a due form of government both civil and ecclesiastical."[38] In such endeavors, he continued, "the care of the public" must overrule all private interests, "for particular estates cannot subsist in the ruin of the public." The new colonists had entered into covenant with God to perform the work which lay ahead. They had been commissioned for this task, and the Lord had given them permission to draw up their own articles of governance. If they were brought safely to their destination, their covenant would be thereby ratified and their commission sealed by Divine Providence. In consequence God would require a strict performance of the articles contained in the covenant. If the people proved unfaithful, they would be punished. The only way to avoid such shipwreck was for the group to be "knit together" as one body in this work and to follow the counsel of the prophet Micah: to do justly, to love mercy, and to walk humbly with their God.[39] Recalling Moses' last farewell to Israel (Deut.30), Winthrop exhorted the people to be obedient to the commandments of God and to the articles of the covenant which they had made with God. To do so was to choose life and prosperity; to disobey was to choose death and destruction.

JUSTICE AND VIRTUE

In an effort to clarify the relationships of justice to law and virtue in covenantal thought, it is useful to recall the connections between these ideas in the classical tradition of moral philosophy. The same fundamental elements of justice are present in both traditions; at the same time, however, the covenantal and classical ideas of justice represent different underlying conceptions of moral agency. For Aristotle and Aquinas justice is understood primarily in terms of virtue. Justice, Aristotle declared, is distinguished from all of the other virtues in that it alone is directed toward "the good of others"; it "promotes the interests of somebody else."[40] In its most comprehensive form (legal or general justice), it orders human life toward the good of the community as a whole. In the classical tradition, law is subordinated to virtue, and obedience is subordinated to pursuit of the good. In covenantal thought, justice is fundamentally a matter of obedience to the law of God. Both virtue and the common good are defined in terms of obedience to the divine law. The classical and covenantal traditions employ different primary symbols of justice; yet in each tradition the latter includes elements of law and of virtue, of duty and of aspiration. Viewed from a moral perspective, the great end of covenant theology was to construct a theory of communal responsibility in which law and the good were united, in which the attainment of the good – of blessing and prosperity – was made conditional upon obedience to fundamental moral law.[41]

Both in the covenantal and in the classical traditions, the relationship of justice to virtue is two-fold. As virtue, justice pertains, first of all, to a quality of the agent's character, namely, the disposition to seek "the good of others." It also pertains to the way in which that good is conceived. In its most inclusive sense, justice is directed toward the common good. Virtue pertains both to the orientation of the agent toward the well-being of the community as a whole and to knowledge of what constitutes that well-being. Perkins addressed both of these aspects of justice in a work entitled, *The Whole Treatise of Cases of Conscience.*[42] In this essay Perkins undertook to set forth a doctrine of conscience, based upon Scripture, which would provide comfort and relief to the consciences of persons who were anxious and troubled about their election. A proper doctrine of conscience offered both a basis for assurance of salvation and a source of moral guidance. Perkins' treatise is divided into three books. The first deals with cases of conscience which pertain to individuals considered in themselves apart from their relationships to others. The second deals with cases of conscience which pertain to the individual in relation to God. In the third book Perkins includes all questions of conscience which pertain to human relationships in society, whether in the family, the church, or the commonwealth. All such questions, he believes, can best be treated under the heading of virtue.

Character

For Perkins, virtue is fundamentally a gift of grace rather than a human achievement.[43] This is true both for believers and for non-believers. Wherever virtue exists, it is a gift which flows freely from the spirit of God; nevertheless there is a profound difference between the virtues of non-believers and those of Christians. The virtues of non-believers are restraining virtues only, serving to repress evil for the sake of the common good; in contrast, the virtues of Christians not only serve to restrain evil but also to renew the mind, the will, and the affections of believers.[44] The virtues of non-believers are "general and common to all"; they are gifts of a common grace. The virtues of the elect, however, are special graces. Among non-believers, justice serves to hold evil within bounds; among believers it has a sanctifying and renewing quality. In this respect Perkins' concept of virtue is more closely akin to that of Augustine and Edwards than that of Aquinas. Unless the common virtues are accompanied by a transformation of the affections, they are sinful.[45] In the language of Jonathan Edwards, "true virtue" – virtue in the fullest sense – is part of the work of regeneration.

For Ames, also, virtue is an essential part of that obedience which is acceptable to God.[46] Good works are an expression of virtue whereby the heart "is inclined to that which is good." The works of the unregenerate are morally good in so far as they conform to the law of God; yet in a religious sense they are not good because they lack the quality of "spiritual obedience."[47] Considered as a virtue, justice is – in the words of Perkins – "a conformity of the will, affections and powers of the body to do the will of God."[48] Apart from virtue there is no true justice.

In *The New Covenant* Preston sets forth the relationship between virtue and obedience with exceptional clarity. God's promise of salvation is accompanied by the demand for moral integrity and perfection of the heart.[49] This does not mean, however, that the covenant itself is conditional upon the fulfillment of these demands; on the contrary, the very possibility of fulfilling such demands is dependent on inclusion in the covenant through divine grace, or election. The obedience that is required of the elect for the realization of the promised salvation is faith and repentance; even these, however, are ultimately gifts *before* they are required. The inward abilities, habits, and graces which enable sinners to repent are "planted in us by the power of Christ"; what is required of those who receive these gifts is that they "bring forth fruit" of such graces.[50] Obedience is required, but obedience is the fruit of virtue, and virtue is a gift. Both virtue and obedience are evangelical rather than legal.[51]

The common good

Both in the covenantal and in the classical tradition, justice is directed toward the good of the whole. "Justice is a virtue," Ames declares, "whereby we are inclined to perform all due offices to our neighbor."[52] Charity teaches that in relation to temporal goods, every person is obliged "to prefer a public person" before oneself; for "the good of the whole is more to be valued than the good of any part."[53]

In covenantal thought the primacy of the public good in justice is expressed characteristically in two main ways. Firstly, it is included in the doctrine of vocation. Each person's vocation or calling is ordained by God "for the common good," Perkins declared.[54] All human societies, including churches and common-wealths, are bodies consisting of many members with different callings, each designed to foster the well-being of the whole. The common good of all consists in this, not just that they live, but that "they live well, in righteousness and holiness, and consequently in true happiness." The use of one's vocation to pursue only one's private good is an abuse of one's calling. Or, to put the matter more plainly still, the "common saying, *Every man for himself and God for us all*, is wicked, and is directly against the end of every calling or honest kind of life." For Baxter, also, vocation was a way of doing "the public good."[55] To this end children should be taught "how great a part of their duty lieth in caring for the common good, and how sinful and damnable it is to live only to themselves."

Secondly, the priority of the public good was embodied in the idea of "a holy commonwealth." Human beings are sociable, Baxter declared, both through natural inclination and through necessity. We are created sociable "for the common good ... and principally because ... holy societies honor our maker more than holy separate persons."[56] The Puritan idea of society was characteristically expressed in terms of a commonwealth. "A common-wealth properly so-called," Baxter wrote, "is a society of God's subjects ordered into the relation of sovereign and subjects for the common good and the pleasing of God their Absolute Sovereign."[57] While Baxter preferred a theocracy, he believed that good rulers would make any form of government a blessing to the people. Through their character they would be disposed toward the true ends of government, namely, the honoring of God and the public welfare.

In New England this idea of justice was set forth in an election sermon of Jonathan Mitchell in 1667. Mitchell declared that the duty of civil rulers to seek "the welfare of the people" is based both upon the law of nature and upon Scripture.[58] Laws which are contrary to the public good are not binding upon conscience. Mitchell goes on to identify certain general principles which constitute the welfare of the people: religion, personal and public safety, and participation in "the rules and fruits of righteousness, equity, order and peace." Moreover, there is great need for prudence, he believes, in the application of these principles.[59]

JUSTICE AND LAW: EQUITY

In the covenant between the people and rulers there was common agreement that society was to be governed by the absolute law of God. While this is most fully known through the revealed law of Scripture, it is also present in the natural law discernible through reason. Thus, while magistrates had sworn to govern according to the law of God, they must be guided both by the law of nature and by the revealed law. The covenant between the people and the magistrates was fundamentally a covenant of trust. Hence, it could not be reduced either to the letter of biblical law or to codes of positive law.

Given the common agreement that society should be ruled according to God's law, one of the most difficult questions which magistrates faced was how the law should be applied to the fallen human condition. Perkins attended to this matter in "Epiekeia, or a Treatise of Christian Equity, and Moderation." According to Perkins, equity, or moderation, is a virtue which is essential for peace in every human society. Christian equity may be either public or private.[60] Private equity pertains to the relationship between individuals in their private actions. Public equity, on the other hand, is that form of equity which is practiced in public meetings and assemblies, including courts of justice, councils, and parliaments. It is concerned with "the right and convenient, and the moderate and discreet *execution of the laws of men*."[61] Human laws, made by lawful authority according to God's law and for the common good, are the "bones and sinews" of all societies. Hence, God has given to rulers authority not only to command and execute his own revealed laws but also to enact other laws "for the more particular government of their people" and for assistance in the execution of God's law. In pursuit of their vocation magistrates are given authority to prescribe penalties and inflict punishments for the violation of law. Public equity is concerned with the proper application of the law under particular circumstances.

According to Perkins, public equity includes consideration of two things: the extremity of the law and mitigation of the law. The extremity of the law refers to its strict application in a literal and precise sense without any relaxation of the prescribed penalties for "good and convenient" reasons.[62] When there are no mitigating circumstances, strict application of the law is just. When such conditions are present, however, adherence to the letter of the law is "flat injustice." In these circumstances, the law should be interpreted less rigorously, and the prescribed punishments should be reduced, deferred, or possibly remitted for "good and sufficient reason." Since law-makers cannot deal with all cases which may arise under particular laws, magistrates must exercise discretion in their interpretation and application of the laws. Qualifications of judges include both knowledge of the strict meaning of the law and the virtue of Christian equity.[63] The "glory and beauty" of a commonwealth consists in "the true knowledge and due practice" of equity.

In order to curb evil and maintain a proper respect for authority, a strict application of the positive law must be presumed, Perkins believed. Any deviation from the positive law must therefore be justified on the basis of one or more of the following three criteria; if it is in accordance with the law of nature, if it is in agreement with the moral law or any part of the written word, or if an inferior law is countermanded by a higher law. Under any of the foregoing circumstances, moderation of the law and mitigation of punishment is "honest, profitable, and convenient." It is not only permissible; it is also obligatory.

The purpose of moderation is the reformation of the criminal. Justice and mercy are sisters; they always go hand in hand.[64] One cannot exist apart from the other. In contrast to the absolute law of God, human laws are imperfect; this is the primary reason why equity is needed in the execution of all positive law. The law, or word, of God includes both the extremity and the mitigation of law, both strict application and leniency. If they are just, human laws must therefore also contain both of these elements. In order that evil may be more effectively restrained, however, only the extremity is specified in the positive law. The demand for equity is, nevertheless, also present by implication in the intent of all just human laws.[65] Yet the demand for equity does not finally rest upon the human law itself, but rather upon the command of God. The law of God is "the fountain of equity"; it also contains the norms of equity. In order to discern what equity requires, magistrates must be guided by a sensitive conscience.

Perkins wrote in a period when equity was understood as "a set of principles which supplemented the common law and modified its inequities."[66] It was administered by the Chancellor, who was regarded as "the keeper of the king's conscience" because he ruled according to conscience instead of precedent. The Court of Chancery was similarly called a "court of conscience." Equity procedures applied particularly to cases of fraud, breach of trusts, wrongs and oppressions. By the end of the sixteenth century, the claims of equity were expressed in a number of maxims, or principles, which served to moderate the rigor and the abstraction of the civil law. In *Epiekeia*, Perkins sought to develop the idea of equity "as laid down by Aristotle and Aquinas within the framework of Reformed theology."[67] For Perkins, equity was an essential quality of justice. Unlike Aquinas, however, he based the claim of equity, not on natural law, but on the Word of God.[68]

In an influential treatise on *Conscience*, William Ames similarly distinguished between strict legal justice and equity. In that work Ames acknowledged his indebtedness to Perkins. Just laws always have two ends, he wrote. One end is intrinsic and immediate; the other, extrinsic and more remote.[69] Strict legal justice is limited to the immediate aim and letter of the law; equity is principally concerned with the ultimate end and the intent of the law. Justice in the fullest sense is equity; apart from equity, legal justice is "iniquity." Most importantly, both for Perkins and for Ames magistrates have a responsibility for the administration of equity as well as strict justice.

As governor of Massachusetts, Winthrop embodied the Puritan ideals of magistracy as a calling and justice as equity. Magistrates are chosen by the people, he declared; but their authority is from God. In their covenant with the people, they have sworn to govern and judge by the laws of God and their own statutes according to their best skills.[70] Like Perkins, by whom he was strongly influenced, Winthrop argued for wide discretion on the part of magistrates and judges in the application of civil law. The prescription of fixed punishments prevents the use of law for admonition, and it leaves no place for wisdom and mercy. Moreover, penalties are not always prescribed even in Scripture.[71] Law is natural to humanity; penalty is positive and accidental. Although prescribed penalties are needed in some instances, they are frequently a source of oppression and injustice. Winthrop did not condemn fixed punishments altogether but only insofar as they conflict with "the rules of justice, and prudence, and mercy" or with the discretionary power of judges.[72]

JUSTICE AS A PUBLIC TRUST

Thus far we have been considering a number of important elements in the Puritan covenantal tradition of justice. Among these are the presupposition of a transcendent moral order, the notion of covenant as the fundamental bond of society, the priority of the public good over private interest, and the necessity of virtue for the practice of justice. We are now in a position to ask whether there is any underlying image of justice that holds these elements together. If so, does this image issue in a distinctive conception of justice? Finally, how is this conception of justice related to notions of justice based on natural law, a social contract, or legal positivism?

The Puritan doctrine of a conditional covenant included two fundamental ideas, namely, the absoluteness of the divine law and the necessity of human moral activity to attain the promised benefits of the covenant. Humanity is required to obey the divinely established law. Such law is the measure of all human justice. But whereas the strict Calvinists interpreted the divine law positivistically in terms of the commandments revealed in Scripture, covenantal writers such as Perkins and Winthrop argued for a larger role for equity in the application of revealed law and in the enactment of civil law.

For Jonathan Mitchell, the law of God enjoins that "civil affairs be managed according to right reason and equity."[73] Although the elect were able, on the basis of grace, to enter into compacts with God and with one another based upon mutual agreements, such compacts presupposed the absoluteness of the law of God. The Puritans who settled in Massachusetts were commissioned to establish a commonwealth in New England. While they were permitted, under the covenant, to enact their own legislation, this freedom was limited by the oath which they had taken to obey the divine law. Moral responsibility and accountability were incorporated into the very substance of grace. Moral obligation presupposed freedom to consent to the rule of law; but it did not presuppose freedom to determine, or even to negotiate, what constitutes the fundamental moral law.

Like Calvin, the Puritans maintained a sense of the mystery and freedom of God both in his ultimate being and in his relationship to the world. Even when they appealed to the law of nature as a criterion of the law of God, such claims referred to God's condescension – his gracious agreement – to enter into covenant with humanity based upon the "light of reason"; such claims did not refer to the unsearchable mystery and character of God in his final transcendence over the world.[74] In this respect the federal theologians differed from Anglican rationalists such as Jeremy Taylor, who insisted that the divine justice is subject to the same laws of reason as human justice. According to Taylor, God was not free to establish rules of justice that are contrary to human perceptions of them, for he was bound by the same laws of reason as any other rational being. In contrast, the Puritan theologians of the covenant maintained only that God had freely agreed to be bound by the law of nature, or reason, in the covenant which he had instituted with humanity.

From a pragmatic standpoint, there might seem to be little or no difference between the Puritan and the Anglican rationalists concerning the nature of justice in human affairs. In reality, however, the difference is profound, for the Puritans' concept of the mystery and transcendence of God contained the basis for new understandings of justice based upon new disclosures of the divine will. Viewed in terms of the creative and ordering activity of God in history, all systems of justice are partial embodiments of the claims of justice. Viewed in terms of the transcendence and judgment of God, they are also manifestations of injustice based upon sin.

What, then, is justice in Puritan covenantal thought? In a formal sense, justice may be defined as obedience to the laws of God. Both the divine law revealed in Scripture and human law that is based upon right reason are included in the law of God. As we have seen, however, justice in human affairs is not strict application of the letter of the law. Justice must be accompanied by equity in the interpretation and application of the written law. Moreover, private interests must be subordinated to the public good.

Equity is essentially a moral principle based upon the character of the ruling authorities. In addition to knowledge of the law, the rulers need the virtues of prudence and discretion in the interpretation and execution of the law. A good ruler, Willard wrote, must have the capacity for disinterested judgment and be devoted to the public good.[75] For the Puritans, magistracy was fundamentally a trust. It was a vocation which depended upon character as well as upon knowledge of the law and principles of justice. It depended finally upon a sensitive conscience – that is, upon a conscience that was instructed by the law of God and formed by virtue.

Since the purpose of civil government was the promotion of the public good, justice necessarily included the primacy of the public good over all private interests. Commitment to the common good was an essential quality both of just laws and of just rulers. Moreover, both of the latter are necessary for the achievement of the public good. "Laws of men, made by lawful authority according to God's law, and for the common good, are, and are to be esteemed, bones and sinews to hold together, props, and pillars, to uphold the commonwealth, and all societies," Perkins declared.[76] Equity was needed to prevent injustice in the administration even of just laws; but equity in turn was limited by the common good.

RIGHTS AND LIBERTIES

In the debates about equity, Winthrop argued for minimal legislation in the Colony of Massachusetts and for larger space for discretion on the part of magistrates and judges in the execution of law and justice. Almost from the beginning, however, the freemen of Massachusetts pressed for the enactment of a code of laws which would guarantee the protection of their civil rights and liberties. John Cotton and Nathaniel Ward, both prominent members of the clergy, were leaders in this movement and participated in the drafting of "The Massachusetts Body of Liberties," which was enacted into law by the General Court in 1641.[77] The code itself was essentially a bill of rights to protect the people of the Colony from arbitrary government; it was not a defense of popular government. Neither Cotton nor Ward believed in the latter. Both agreed that, due to the corruption of human nature, all government should be limited; otherwise it would result in tyranny. Moreover, the best form of limitation was a public declaration of the rights of the subjects – of those rights and liberties which are "due to every man in his place and proportion without impeachment and infringement." The peace and stability, both of churches and of commonwealths, depend upon the honoring and exercising of these liberties.

It is important to see the Body of Liberties in the context of the seventeenth century. Viewed in that light, this document expressed a fundamental equality and liberty of all persons within the framework of a hierarchically structured social order. Some of the liberties applied equally to all persons residing within the Colony, including foreigners. Others pertained particularly to members of certain groups or classes such as freemen, women, children, servants, and foreigners. The enactment of these freedoms into law was a public affirmation of the fundamental dignity of all persons, and a commitment to human rights based upon that dignity. Through the action of the General Court the freemen of the Colony covenanted together that these liberties and privileges would be "impartially and inviolably enjoyed and observed throughout our jurisdiction forever."[78] The same justice and the same law applied to every person within the jurisdiction of the Colony.

Equality did not yet mean equal participation of all members of society in popular democratic government. In Massachusetts and New Haven the franchise was restricted to church members. While suffrage was not expressly confined to members of the churches in the Connecticut settlements, there the electorate was under the supervision of the clergy; thus, the same control by the churches was achieved by more indirect means.[79] Under the first

charter of Massachusetts only about one fifth of the total population were granted franchise. Yet the ideas of a fundamental
equality (dignity) and liberty (consent) were implicit in Puritan
covenantal thought. The notion of liberties which extended to all
persons, including foreigners and strangers, rested upon an
underlying dignity which was shared by all. The right of liberty
was expressed in covenant as consent to governance. It was also
expressed in the participation of the freemen in elections, in the
accountability of the officers of the colony, and in the safeguards
against tyranny which were embodied in the law.

The forms which these ideas took in the eighteenth century did
not so much represent a break with Puritan covenantal thought
as they did the development and reformulation of these concepts
in democratic and secular terms.[80] According to its original
charter, the members of the Massachusetts Bay Company had
been granted full power to legislate for the colony and to establish
whatever form of government they chose over the settlers. In the
establishment of "a due form of government," however, Winthrop initiated a series of changes in the charter which resulted in
the adoption of a constitution by the people and the admission of
a larger portion of the colonists to the rank of freemen. While
these alterations did not issue in a fully democratic form of
government, they are nonetheless astonishing. Through them the
trading company was transformed into a commonwealth.[81] The
function of the "assistants" was transformed from an executive
committee, elected by members of the company, into a legislative
assembly; and the term "freemen" was transformed from a
designation for the members of a trading company into citizens of
a state with the right to vote and hold office. The fundamental
reason for these changes, Morgan suggests, was rooted in Winthrop's understanding of the covenantal basis of all forms of
human community, including both church and state.[82] "It is of
the nature and essence of every society," Winthrop declared, "to
be knit together by some covenant, either expressed or implied."
Hence, the "due form of government" which God had commissioned the new settlers in Massachusetts to establish must be
created by a voluntary compact between the rulers and the
subjects.

In the eighteenth century the idea of the covenant underwent many developments. The concept itself came to be restated largely in terms of a secular covenant between rulers and the subjects, and attention was focused increasingly upon the purpose of the state in terms of the mutual protection of the lives, liberties, and properties of the people. More and more the ideas of inviolable rights, resistance to tyrants, and the right of revolution were advanced and defended on rational grounds by the New England ministers. In so doing John Wise, Elisha Williams, Jonathan Mayhew, Samuel Langdon, and Ezra Stiles were developing the implications of Puritan covenantal thought, in response to the changing political climate in the colonies and to the new forms of political philosophy which were taking shape in Europe.[83] By the time of the Revolution, government by consent, limitation of the power of government, and participation of the people in governance were all included in the covenant between the rulers and the people. These ideas were, of course, central to Locke's notion of a social compact; moreover, Locke's treatises on civil government had influenced the development of Puritan thought on these matters in the course of the eighteenth century. Both the Puritans and Locke defended the notion of government by consent on the basis of reason; both also argued for human liberties which existed prior to the state and were grounded upon reason. "The only novelty in Locke's explanation of the formation of government," Morgan suggests, "was the apparent absence of God from the proceedings."[84] Though Locke did not mention God as a participant either in the creation of the social compact or in the establishment of government, "he did identify God as the author of the laws of nature." Not only did these laws precede the formation of government; government itself was bound by them. Both for the Puritans and for Locke, the purpose of government included protection of the lives, liberties, and properties of the people. For both, moreover, the purpose of such protection was the promotion of "the public good."[85]

Despite the growing secularization of the covenant idea and the tendency to re-interpret the latter in contractual terms, the covenantal notions of community and justice were not finally reducible to a social contract. Covenant rested upon a communal conception of human nature; in contrast, the notion of a social contract was fundamentally individualistic. Although Locke was widely interpreted in contractualist terms, his idea of a social compact rested ultimately upon a deeper, underlying notion of covenant. Not only for Puritanism, but also for Locke, the relationship between magistrates and the people is based finally upon trust.[86] In order to gain a clearer understanding of Locke's relation to Puritanism, we turn now to a consideration of his teaching concerning the origins of civil society and the nature of justice.

CHAPTER 5

John Locke: justice and the social compact

The last generation of Lockean scholarship has witnessed a radical reappraisal of the traditional interpretation of Locke as a secular political thinker, a defender of individualism, and a champion of the natural right of private property. The new picture of Locke which has emerged through these more recent studies is the result of an attempt to interpret his various writings in their historical context. The appearance of John Dunn's *The Political Thought of John Locke* in 1969 marked a critical turning-point in the evolution of the historical approach to Lockean studies. Building upon the work of von Leyden, Laslett, and Abrams, Dunn sought to interpret Locke in terms of Locke's own intentions and self-understanding. The single most important key to a recovery of Locke's own intentionality, Dunn argued, was a recognition of the "centrality" of his underlying religious commitments to his thought as a whole.[1]

Since the appearance of Dunn's essay, the fundamental significance of Locke's religious beliefs for his moral and political thought has been generally acknowledged.[2] Assuming the validity of this hypothesis, Locke's rationalism must now be seen within the framework of his religious convictions. Locke attempted to resolve the tension between the two in terms of the law of nature; but, for him, moral obligation remained ultimately dependent upon religious faith in God as Creator and upon an understanding of humanity as God's workmanship.

In recent years a number of scholars, dealing with particular aspects of Locke's work, have attempted to place his economic and political writings in their historical context. Some of these studies have focused upon the development of Locke's thought

80

as evidenced by the texts themselves together with his journal entries. On the basis of a careful textual analysis, Laslett concluded that Locke wrote the *Two Treatises* between 1679 and 1681 and that they were conceived in Locke's mind as a demand for a revolution-yet-to-be rather than as a justification of the Revolution of 1688.[3] Employing a similar type of analysis, Tully has brought to light the communal and potentially radical implications of Locke's concept of property.[4] He has also noted the similarity of Locke's concept of property to that of Aquinas.

Some of these studies, as well as related ones, have also focused intentionally upon the historical setting of Locke's writings – the particular audiences which he addressed, the revolutionary activities in which he participated, and the ways in which he was understood both by his contemporaries and by himself.[5] Ashcraft makes clear the close relationship between Locke's own writings and his association with Shaftesbury and the Puritan Dissenters in the common struggle against tyranny and political absolutism. Many of the basic concepts to which Locke appealed to justify resistance – law of nature, natural rights, and the public good – were already in common use among the Dissenters.

Taken together such studies have resulted in a new appreciation of the religious, the communal, and the radical features of Locke's thought. They have also provided insight into his political and moral ideas, which have their roots in classical medieval thought, as well as in Calvinism and the left-wing Protestantism of seventeenth-century England. Viewed in the light of his own historical situation and his stated religious and moral presuppositions, it becomes apparent that the image of Locke as a champion of unfettered individualism, political rationalism, and liberal bourgeois economics is a caricature of his own moral vision. That there are strong tendencies toward individualism, rationalism, and conservatism in Locke is indisputable, but along with these there is also clear recognition of the communal and religious dimensions of human existence as well as the claims of egalitarianism. Locke's concept of justice includes all dimensions of his thought: the rational and the religious, the individual and the communal, the conservative and also the radical.

THE LAW OF NATURE

From his earliest writings onward Locke was concerned with the basis and nature of political obligation. Although his views as to the precise content which this entailed changed radically after he left Oxford and joined the household of Anthony Ashley Cooper, the first Earl of Shaftesbury, Locke consistently held that the obligation of political obedience was grounded in the duty to obey God. He also held that the divine will is revealed through nature and can thus be discerned by reason. While reason is able to discern the content of the moral law, the duty to obey it rests not upon reason but upon the fact that God is its author. Thus, for Locke, the concept of the law of nature affirmed both the rationality of the moral law and its divine sanction.

While Locke never fully developed the notion of the law of nature, he employed it throughout his writings to establish an objective universal foundation for his moral theory. In two early tracts on the civil magistrate he used this idea to vindicate the duty of absolute obedience to civil authorities and to refute the claim for toleration based upon appeals to conscience.[6] Subsequently, in *Essays on the Law of Nature* he distinguished this concept from the doctrine of innate ideas and from notions of obligation based on the general consent of humanity, tradition, and individual interest. Instead, he argued that the law of nature is an objective moral rule which can be known by reason operating through sense-experience. Such a law is morally binding; it is both eternal and universal. God is the "guarantor" of this moral order and also "the epistemological key" to its proper understanding.[7] In the *Essays* as in the earlier tracts on the civil magistrate, Locke appealed to the law of nature to "affirm an 'official' ethic of authority." While Locke's opinions about the substantive content of the law of nature subsequently changed, he never relinquished the view that the moral authority of the latter rested upon the relationship between God the Creator and his Creation. The essential problem implicit in Locke's early treatment of the law of nature was that of determining how his theological grounding of a universal moral order was related to the epistemological question of identifying the substantive content of that order through reason. This, as Dunn suggests, remained the central unresolved question in Locke's ethical thought.[8]

As suggested above, Locke sought to resolve this problem at the practical level by ascribing the law of nature to God who is its author and who reveals himself through the light of reason as well as through revelation. In *An Essay on Human Understanding* he expressed his belief that "morality is capable of demonstration"; yet he never succeeded in producing such a science of morals.[9] In *The Reasonableness of Christianity* he turned, instead, to revelation for a definitive disclosure of the precepts of morality.[10]

Locke's primary aim in employing the idea of the law of nature was to establish a foundation upon which to construct a moral theory. Although his interpretation of this idea differed in a number of respects from the classical natural law tradition, particularly regarding the nature of good and evil, it nevertheless provided a rational basis for his moral and political thought. In *Two Treatises of Government* it served both as a declaration of God's will through reason and as the criterion of right and wrong.[11] This law "obliges every one"; it wills both "the peace and the preservation of all mankind" [II.6,7]. Though unwritten, it is "plain and intelligible to all rational creatures" [II.124]. Most importantly, its obligations "cease not in society" [II.135]. The obligations of truthfulness and promise-keeping, for example, belong "to men, as men, and not as members of society" [II.14]. Similarly, it is the law of nature, existing prior to any positive civil laws, which limits the amount of private property which individuals can rightfully possess.

NATURAL RIGHTS

Locke's *Two Treatises* was an attack upon arbitrary and absolutist government. The initial stimulus for his assault was a series of political tracts written by Sir Robert Filmer as a Royalist defense of absolute monarchy. These tracts, originally published between 1648 and 1653, were republished in 1679 and again in 1680 on the occasion of the Exclusion Crisis.[12] *Patriarcha*, Filmer's major work, also appeared in 1680, and soon became the primary target of Locke's attack.

Although *Two Treatises* was not published until 1690, Locke had apparently begun work on the former by 1679.[13] The *First Treatise* in particular was intended as a full refutation of Filmer's argument in defense of patriarchy. In the *Second Treatise* Locke undertook a positive statement of his own theory of government. While the specific foci of the two essays are thus different, the themes of patriarchy and absolute monarchy run throughout both. Locke's immediate purpose in publishing *Two Treatises* was to establish the legitimacy of King William III: "to make good his title, in the consent of the people ... and to justify to the world, the people of England, whose love of their just and natural rights, with their resolution to preserve them, saved the nation when it was on the very brink of slavery and ruin."[14]

It has just been noted that the *First Treatise* was primarily a refutation of Filmer's argument in *Patriarcha*. According to Filmer, the claim of absolute monarchy rested ultimately upon Adam's paternal and regal power. The first of these stemmed from Adam's role in the begetting of children; the second was grounded in the dominion which God granted to Adam over the rest of Creation. This authority was inherited, Filmer argued, through a royal line of succession from Adam to the present. Absolute monarchical power rests fundamentally upon the absolute power which Adam had over his children by right of fatherhood and in the absolute dominion over the work of Creation which he had by divine authorization.

As Locke perceived the matter, Filmer's system could be summarized in two concise theses: (1) "That all government is absolute monarchy" and (2) "That no man is born free." Filmer had based his argument largely upon an appeal to Scripture, but he had also appealed on occasion to a natural law argument (i.e., Adam's paternal authority over his children). In opposition to Filmer's claim that Adam had received private dominion over the earth and other living creatures, Locke argued that such dominion had been granted to Adam "in common with the rest of mankind" [1.29]. This right "cannot justly be denied." Not only had God not given Adam private dominion over the earth and other forms of life; the Creator had clearly not given Adam sovereignty either over his children or over Eve. Such power – or authority – over one's own person can be granted only by compact [1.43].

Against Filmer, Locke argues that men are born free and equal [1.67]. They are endowed with "natural liberty and equality." Locke goes to great pains to demolish Filmer's Scriptural argument for absolute monarchy, but his own argument rests fundamentally upon the law of nature, particularly the duty of self-preservation [1.86]. This law is known through the "senses and reason", which is the "voice of God" in humanity. It is "at one and the same time a command of God, a rule of reason, and a law in the very nature of things as they are, by which they work and we work too."[15]

For a fuller account of Locke's concept of natural rights, we turn now to the *Second Treatise*. For Locke, natural rights are grounded upon duties which are implicit in the laws of nature.[16] The "fundamental law of nature" is "the preservation of mankind" [11.135]. This law gives rise to two basic duties; to preserve oneself and to preserve others. Locke bases the law of preservation of mankind upon two main arguments. The first is derived from an understanding of humanity as God's workmanship [11.6]. As God's workmanship, men are "sent into the world by his order and about his business, they are his property ... made to last during his, not one another's pleasure." Everyone is therefore "bound to preserve himself"; and, to the extent possible within this limit, everyone ought "to preserve the rest of mankind." A second argument in support of this primary law of nature is based upon the purposive relationship between man and his physical environment.[17] God has implanted a strong desire for self-preservation in man. He has, moreover, "furnished the world with things fit" for the necessities of life [11.86]. Having made man and the world thus, God directed man through his senses and reason, to use those things "which were serviceable for his subsistence" and which had been "given him as means of his preservation." The suitability of the world for man's preservation was an argument based upon God's design in Creation. This argument presupposed that humanity is God's workmanship; it also demonstrated the rationality of the obligation to preserve mankind.

While the entire natural law is in a certain sense included in
the duty to preserve mankind, Locke also speaks of "the preservation of society" as a law of nature [II.134]. In contrast to Hobbes,
Locke presupposes that man is by nature a "sociable creature"
and that he is unable to exist apart from society. Hence, it follows
that man has a duty to preserve society. God placed man "under
strong obligations of necessity, convenience, and inclination to
drive him into society"; he also provided man "with understanding and language to continue and enjoy it" [II.77]. The
obligation to preserve society is, in short, derived by reason from
man's natural dependence upon society and the primary obligation to preserve oneself and others.[18] Since human beings do not
and cannot exist apart from society, there is an obligation,
discernible by reason, to preserve society and also to fulfill those
duties upon which the continued existence of society depends.
Pre-eminent among such duties is promise–keeping. The latter is
prerequisite for the existence of any society; hence, it is grounded
in natural law. As such it is universally acknowledged within –
although not between – all societies.[19] So great is the obligation
to keep promises and oaths that even the Almighty is bound by
them [II.195].

For Locke natural rights are correlative with duties enjoined by
the law of nature. These are essentially claims which all people
have for those conditions and resources which are necessary for
the fulfillment of the obligations of the law of nature. As we have
seen, these obligations continue in conventional, or political,
society. Since they impose duties upon humankind, they imply
natural rights claims to those circumstances which are necessary
for their fulfillment. Locke identifies three such natural rights: life,
liberty, and possessions (property) [II.135].[20]

All three of these basic rights are grounded in the fundamental
law of nature, that "mankind ought to be preserved." By this
phrase Locke does not mean merely that the human species
should be kept from extinction; he means that the life of every
individual ought to be protected in this way: "Men, being once
born, have a right to their preservation" [II.25]. The right to self-
preservation is a "native and original right"; it belongs both to
individuals [II.149] and to societies [II.220]. Men "will always

have a right to preserve what they have not a power to part with [i.e., their own lives]; and to rid themselves of those who invade this fundamental, sacred, and unalterable law of self-preservation" [II.149]. Along with the right to self-preservation, Locke affirms the right to engage in those activities which are necessary for the preservation of mankind, including both oneself and others.

In *Two Treatises*, Locke appeals to these two fundamental rights – the right to preservation and the right to preserve mankind – to justify resistance to arbitrary and absolute rule. Since the former are grounded in the universal obligation to preserve mankind, they imply a common positive duty to resist all arbitrary attempts to destroy either oneself or others.[21] Such resistance may take the form of punishing offenders; demanding reparation if one is injured; or, in political societies, resisting unjust rulers [II.8,11,232].

A third natural right is also based upon the rights which all men have to preserve both themselves and others, namely, a right to "meat and drink, and such other things, as nature affords for their subsistence" [II.25]. Since each person has a right to self-preservation, each also has a right to those things which are essential for survival. Locke sometimes speaks of this right in terms of "possessions" [II.6] or goods [II.173]; more characteristically, he uses the term "property" to include not only material possessions but also "that property which men have in their persons" [II.173]. In this broad sense "property" includes men's "lives, liberties, and estates" [II.123; cf.221].[22]

The rights which these various forms of property entail will be considered more fully when we turn to Locke's concept of property. At this point it is sufficient to note that Locke distinguishes between two fundamentally different kinds of property. On the one hand, the right which all persons have in common to the goods of nature is an "inclusive" right. On the other, the rights which each person has both in his private possessions and in his own person are "exclusive" rights. None of these rights is absolute, for all are limited by duties imposed by the law of nature. The exclusive right to private possessions is limited, for example, by the duty to preserve others (mankind). Similarly, while everyone has an exclusive property in his own person, "no body has an arbitrary power over himself" [II.27; 135]. Hence, no one has a right "to destroy his own life" or "to subject himself to the arbitrary power of another." In the ultimate sense, mankind is God's property [II.6]. Men belong to the Creator, for they are his workmanship; and they are obliged to do his will.

THE SOCIAL COMPACT

In the state of nature all men are free and equal [II.4,6]. Within the limits of the law of nature they are free "to order their actions, and dispose of their possessions, and persons as they think fit." They are also equal; the power and jurisdiction which they have over each other is reciprocal and mutual.[23] All are bound by the same law, the law of nature. All have the same basic obligations, and all are bearers of the same natural rights, including the executive power of the law of nature [II.8,13].

Not only are all men born free and equal. They are also rational. Reason is "the common bond whereby human kind is united into one fellowship and society" [II.172]. It is "the common rule and measure" of human action [II.11]. Anyone who abandons and replaces it with the rule of force behaves like an animal and may be treated as such. As Laslett observes, reason is "the mode of co-operation between men."[24] It is the basis both of society and of security [II.172]. Such rationality, it should be noted, is closely linked with Locke's individualism. Not only are all men equal in terms of the natural law; their relationship to that law is conceived individualistically. This is true both of each persons's perception of the law of nature and also of the right which each has to enforce the latter. "Reason ... teaches ... that being all equal and independent, no one ought to harm another in his life, health, liberty, or possessions" [II.6]. The authority of the law of nature must be finally discerned by each person through reason, not through tradition or on the basis of convention.

The state of nature is not a historical concept but, rather, "a jural condition."[25] "All men are naturally in that state, and remain so," Locke declares, "till by their own consents they make themselves members of some (political) society" [II.15]. The state of nature was an analytic construct which Locke used to establish a normative foundation for government as well as the limits of legitimate political power. In the state of nature all men are free, equal and independent. Nevertheless, humanity is also social by nature. In creation God placed man "under strong obligations of necessity, convenience, and inclination to drive him into society" [II.77].[26] The Creator also endowed him with reason and language suited to that end.

The state of nature differs sharply both from a state of war and from political society. The first society, which existed in man's natural state, was "between man and wife" [II.77]. This, in turn, became the basis for the community of parents and children. Conjugal society rested principally upon the biological dependence of the sexes in procreation; it was also nurtured by the common desire for mutual support and ties of tenderness and affection. For Locke the natural state of mankind is "a state of peace, good will, mutual assistance, and preservation" [II.19]. It is a condition in which men live together "according to reason, without a common superior on earth, with authority to judge between them."

Despite all of its privileges, however, the state of nature is but "an ill condition" [II.127]. It is characterized by insecurity, anxiety, and other inconveniences. These conditions have been compounded by the Fall.[27] Three things in particular are wanting in man's natural state: an established, known law; a known and indifferent judge; and power to enforce the law [II.124–126]. Thus men are driven by necessity, convenience, and inclination to establish governments and political societies [II.77,127]. Their primary purpose in so doing is "the mutual preservation of their lives, liberties, and estates," all of which Locke includes in the general term "property." In short, men form political societies in order to preserve their property [II.124]. Locke states this purpose both in individualistic terms and in terms of the public good. In entering civil society each person intends to find greater security for his own life, liberty, and property within the restraints imposed by the good of the whole. At the same time, however, Locke states succinctly that the only proper end of government is "the peace, safety, and publick good of the people" [II.131]. Despite the strongly individualistic features of his anthropology, the tension between individualism and the requirements of collective life remains unresolved.

The problem which Locke addressed in *Two Treatises* was not that of explaining the origins of society but, rather, the origins of civil society and the limits of legitimate political power. Men enter political society whenever they consent to form a community in which they give up their individual power of punishment, delegate this power to a common judge, and agree to live under a common body of law [II.97,127]. Locke calls such an agreement a compact.[28] All that the latter requires is the bare agreement "to unite into one political society" [II.99; cf. II.14]. The only rightful basis for the formation of such societies, Locke argues, lies in consent. The same is also true of all lawful government. That "which begins and actually *constitutes any political society*, is nothing but the consent of any number of freemen capable of a majority to unite and incorporate into such a society. And this is that, and that only, which did, or could give *beginning* to any *lawful government* in the world" [II.99].

Although civil society and government are both based fundamentally in consent, Locke distinguishes between the processes whereby the two are formed. The civil community comes into being through a compact; government, on the other hand, comes into being through the establishment by the community of a common ruling authority and the entrustment of political power to the latter.[29] While the two processes may take place at the same time, they are nevertheless distinct. The formation of a civil compact refers to the creation of a community. The establishment of government refers to an action of that community as a whole regarding the conferral of political power, which includes both legislative and executive power. Although the legislative is superior to the executive power, both are fiduciary in nature.[30] Both are limited by the ends for which political society is established, namely, the preservation of the lives, liberties, and properties of the people. Supreme power remains in the people. They retain the right either to remove or to alter the legislative body when it acts contrary to its trust [II.149]. They also retain a similar right to resist, and even to overthrow, rulers under similar circumstances [II.156,242]. In short, all political power rests upon the "explicit or tacit trust" that it shall be used for the good of the people and for the preservation of their property [II.171].

Though all political power rests upon consent, natural law imposes certain limits even upon the power to consent. For example, since no one possesses arbitrary power over his own life, no one is able to grant such authority to any other person [II.172]. The law of self-preservation continues to oblige in civil society. Since this obligation entails the means which are essential to its fulfillment, no one can grant to another absolute control over his property. Moreover, since self-preservation is a positive duty, men will always have a right to overthrow those who infringe this "unalterable law." The right of the people to resist tyranny is absolute, for supreme political power resides in them.[31]

JUSTICE

Although the concept of justice is not treated at length in any of Locke's completed works, it is a major underlying theme throughout his political thought as a whole.[32] While he does not provide a developed concept of a just society, he does present a structure for justice, including both transcendent and conventional justice. The former is grounded in the law of nature; it is also universal. The latter is based in positive law; as such it is relative to particular societies. For Locke, natural justice sets the limits and provides the basic direction for civic justice through the concept of natural rights. At its most fundamental level, Locke's theory of justice is a natural law rather than natural rights theory. While certain rights are inclusive and inalienable, they are nevertheless based upon, and limited by, the law of nature.[33]

In order to understand Locke's concept of justice, it is necesary to look briefly at the evolution of this idea in his thought as a whole. His earliest political writings were a staunch defense of authoritarianism. In *Two Tracts on Government* Locke argues that, since God willed that there be "order, society and government among men", there must be some supreme power in every commonwealth.[34] The magistrate is accountable only to God. He has sovereign power over "all indifferent things," including the possessions of the subjects. In this early period Locke implicitly rejects any natural right to property. Property is essentially a private right, but as such it can be changed or abolished by order of the magistrate at any time.[35]

In *Essays on the Law of Nature* Locke deals more extensively with the notion of justice. He calls it the "chief law of nature and bond of every society."[36] Justice is inconceivable without personal property because it pertains primarily to the distribution of goods.[37] Justice means the security of each person's personal possessions as a right based upon the law of nature.[38]

In the *Essays* Locke based the right to private property on the law of nature, but he did not use this law as a basis for a critique of the positive law and political absolutism. In the 1667 *Essay on Toleration*, however, he made an important initial move in this direction when he argued that it is unjust for magistrates to impose restrictions upon the moral behavior of individuals unless such restraints are necessary to protect the public welfare. More particularly, the right of the magistrate to alter property arrangements is now limited by his duty to promote the general good.[39] If the magistrate transgresses this moral limit, passive obedience remains a duty, for subjects have no right of resistance. But as Dunn observes, this shift from Locke's defense of political absolutism, while slight in terms of its immediate application, was nonetheless critical. It constituted a moral criterion in terms of which magistrates could be judged even though it did not yet establish a legal or constitutional basis for calling them to accountability.

In the 1671 drafts of *An Essay Concerning Human Understanding*, Locke undertook an epistemological analysis of moral ideas. Such ideas, he declared, consist of two general kinds of moral norms or rules. Firstly, there are conventional notions of virtue and vice based upon common usage in various societies; secondly, there are norms based upon rules or laws that have been set by a superior power.[40] Locke calls those actions which are commanded or forbidden by God "good or evil, sin or duty"; those which are commanded or forbidden by civil law he calls "lawful or unlawful." Only the former are morally binding or obligatory.

Obedience or disobedience to the divine law brings good or evil upon humanity. In contrast, conventional notions of morality have only linguistic and rhetorical value; they pertain to proper speech, the understanding of virtues and vices, and the attainment of reputation. In the *Essay* true morality, including true justice, is based upon the declared will of a supreme invisible lawgiver, but consideration of how his will and law are made known is deferred by Locke till a fit occasion arises to speak of God and the law of nature.[41]

LOCKE'S CONCEPT OF PROPERTY

In *Two Treatises* Locke returns to the idea of justice, and he does so in terms of the concept of property. Justice, which was treated formally in the *Essay*, is now given substantive content in his discussions of property and resistance to arbitrary rulers. Here Locke addresses the disjuncture between conventional, positive law and true justice based on the law of nature. His answer to this problem lies in the development of a concept of civic justice within limits imposed by the fundamental law of nature. Since this law constitutes the will of the Supreme Lawgiver, it obliges all men, both in the state of nature and in political society. It also establishes the basis for certain human rights, some of which are inalienable and some of which can be given up only by consent.

In *Two Treatises*, it will be recalled, Locke uses the term property in two main senses. In its broadest sense, property includes one's person, action, liberty, life, and estate. "Property" embraces everything which a person has rightful control over and which therefore cannot be taken from him without his own consent [II.193]. On the basis of this understanding of property, Locke identifies three basic rights which belong to all men: the right to self-preservation [II.11], the right of preserving all mankind [II.11,135], and the right to the means necessary for subsistence [II.25]. These are natural rights claims; they are inclusive and inalienable. Locke also refers to these as rights to one's life, liberty, and possessions. All three are included in the general category of property, understood in the broad sense.

Locke also uses the term property in a narrower sense to refer
to the goods, or possessions, which are subject to one's control.
In part, such goods belong to all men in common since God
gave the earth to all; in part, they belong exclusively to
individuals. "Property" in the sense of "possessions" includes
both common and private goods. Locke defines the former as "a
right to" and the latter as "a right in."[42] Accordingly, Locke has
two concepts of property rights: one refers to an inclusive "right
to" the goods which nature provides, and the other to an
exclusive "right in" various forms of private possessions. In
addition to an inclusive "right to" the bounty of nature, every
person has an exclusive "right in" those private possessions
which he acquires through the mixture of his own labor with the
goods which nature provides [II.27].

While the function of civil government is to preserve the lives,
liberties, and properties of its subjects, this duty is set within the
overarching limits imposed by the law of nature. These limits are
defined in terms of duties and rights. This is the context in which
Locke takes up a discussion of property in chapter 5 of the *Second
Treatise*. Significantly, Locke addresses this question of the basis
and limits of property prior to entering upon a discussion of
political, or civil, society in the succeeding section of the *Second
Treatise*. Private property, he contends, is not based either upon
utility or upon self–interest; it rests, rather, upon positive duties
which are grounded in natural law. All men have an equal right
to the common goods which nature affords. Beyond this they also
have a right to appropriate portions of the latter by acts of their
own labor, including gathering, hunting, domesticating, and
cultivating [II.28,30, 32,38]. "Justice gives every man a title to the
product of his honest industry" [I.42].

This same justice which confers upon each person an exclusive
right to the product of his own labor also limits the amount of
such possessions in several important ways. Firstly, no one has a
right to more than he can use [II.32]. Whatever one is unable to
use or enjoy "before it spoils ... belongs to others" [II.31].
Secondly, the right of private property is limited by the subsistence needs of others [I.42]. Those who are in extreme circum-
stance have a "right to the surplage" of goods which others have

accumulated. Justice thus entails not only a right to the product of one's labor; it also entails a duty to assist those in severe need. Charity is, therefore, both a right on the part of the needy and a duty on the part of those who have a surplus. Finally, in the state of nature, there is a third natural limit on the amount of private property that can rightfully be appropriated out of the common storehouse of nature, namely, the requirement that "enough, and as good [be] left in common for others" [II.27].

With the transition to political society, all of men's possessions are submitted to the community for regulation and control [II.120].[43] To retain jurisdiction over one's own property would be contradictory to the very purpose for which individuals in a state of nature unite to form a commonwealth, which is to provide for the mutual security and regulation of their property. In the state of nature all are free and equal. When they form a political community, they do so on the basis of their natural liberty and equality; together they submit their persons and their possessions to the community for regulation and governance for the public good. Since life and liberty are natural rights, the latter can only be *restricted* and that through consent; they cannot be completely surrendered since to do so would be to violate the law of nature. The same may also be said of the inclusive right of all to the goods which nature provides.

Private possessions, however, are a different matter. In the state of nature private property was limited by the proviso that "enough and as good" be left in the commons which nature has made available to all. In the earliest stages of human development the goods of nature were plenteous and remained largely in common. Under such circumstances "it was impossible for any man ... to intrench upon the right of another, or acquire, to himself, a property, to the prejudice of his neighbor" either through acquisition or through consumption [II.36]. In this Golden Age everyone conformed to the demands of the law of nature "by instinct and reason."[44] Following the Fall, however, the transition from a nomadic to a settled agrarian economy and, particularly, the invention of money, gave rise to covetousness, pride, and ambition. These led, in turn, to conflict, and greatly increased the general sense of anxiety and insecurity. One of the major reasons why men first left the state of nature and formed civil societies was to resolve such conflicts. With the formation of political communities, all private possessions are by common agreement subjected to the commonwealth for its jurisdiction and control. Natural property rights are thereby exchanged for conventional rights.

In establishing a political society all of its members agree to be governed henceforth by those laws which the community as a whole enacts through its legislative power. "Men ... in society having property ... have such a right to the goods, which by the law of the community are theirs" that these goods cannot rightfully be taken from them without their consent [II.138]. Locke does not mean that individual property rights are equated finally with positive law, as such rights are neither unconditional nor absolute. On the contrary, their legitimacy is determined, firstly, by the original consent of all when the society was formed and, secondly, by their conformity with the law of nature [II.135]. In political society, as in the state of nature, all have a natural right to the means necessary for a comfortable subsistence; as God's workmanship, they also have a duty and a right to labor in so far as they are able. Distributive justice is based upon the fulfillment of both of these natural rights claims. Since the right to private property is limited by the public good, it is essentially a "use right," not a right of absolute ownership.[45]

In addition to a distributive principle, for Locke justice also includes a compensatory, or retributive, principle. Compensatory justice may take the form either of reparation or restraint. Both are rights, and both are grounded in the fundamental right of preservation of oneself and others [II.11]. In the state of nature, the right of punishing crime for restraint and protection belongs to everyone. In conventional society this right is given over to the magistrate, who by virtue of his office may either exact or, on occasion, remit the latter for the public good. The right of taking reparation, on the other hand, belongs only to the injured party. Hence, only the person who has suffered damage has a right to demand reparation or the power to forgo the latter [II.11].

In comparison with distributive and compensatory justice, the role of general, or legal, justice is much more problematic.[46] This difficulty is due to a number of factors. It arises mainly out of Locke's method of analyzing moral ideas as distinctive rational concepts separate from their embodiment in moral experience. It is due in part, also, to the ahistoric character of the state of nature as a juridical idea, so that its precise relationship to conventional society frequently remains unclear. The law of nature continues to bind in political society, but the manner in which it binds is subject to various interpretations, especially regarding "indifferent things." In addition, it must be recognized that Locke is not always consistent in his analysis of particular ideas such as property, justice, and charity. His views concerning political absolutism changed radically after he wrote *Two Tracts*. Similarly, his views on toleration and the right of resistance also changed.[47] Finally, the problem of determining the role of general justice in Locke is greatly compounded by his inability to develop a unified conception of morality on the basis of reason.

In the early *Essays* Locke suggested that there is some "primary and fundamental law" from which all of the rules of morality are derived.[48] Though he continued to hold that conviction throughout his life, he was never able to demonstrate on the basis of reason any single moral rule which might serve as the basis and standard of all other moral precepts. In the *Essays* he called justice "the chief law of nature."[49] Since the precepts of justice are negative, however, the latter does not provide a sufficient basis for those communal virtues – traditionally rooted in the affections – which are also essential for human well-being and happiness. Such virtues are the bonds of social cohesion; they provide the basis for mutual commitment to the public good. While Locke recognized the need for such qualities of character as mutual good will, affection, and generosity, he was unable to derive them either from justice or, more broadly, from the law of nature through reason. As a consequence, there is a marked poverty in his concept of justice in comparison with the resources of the intellectual and moral traditions to which he belonged. In *The Reasonableness of Christianity* he turned to revelation for a fuller disclosure of our moral duties than was presently available on the basis of reason alone.

JUSTICE AND CHARITY

Both the strengths and the weaknesses of Locke's concept of
justice are evident in *Two Treatises*. Here the precepts of justice
are essentially negative; they forbid doing harm to "another in his
life, health, liberty, or possessions" [II.6].[50] The aim of justice,
thus understood, is to enable individuals to pursue their own well-
being and happiness without interference, and thus to preserve
human life. Locke recognizes, however, that other more positive
virtues are also necessary for the fulfillment of man's natural
longing for community [II.101].[51] Thus charity as a positive duty
can be derived from the precept of preservation in the same way
that the precept of justice is derived from the latter. Both justice
and charity are based upon the duty to preserve mankind. "As
justice gives every man a title to the product of his honest industry
... so charity gives every man a title to so much out of another's
plenty, as will keep him from extreme want, where he has no
means to subsist otherwise" [1.42]. Charity is both a right on the
part of the needy and a duty on the part of those who have
"enough and to spare." Justice and charity are complementary
duties. As such they remain fundamentally separate and independent virtues; neither encompasses the other. Such a concept of
charity, it should be noted, is sharply limited; it extends only to
the provision of subsistence for the needy.

    In an unfinished paper entitled "Morality," Locke subse-
quently returned to the question of the relationship of justice to
other virtues which are necessary for human happiness. Once the
basis and nature of justice are established, it would not be hard,
he believed, to establish additional virtues "which relate to society
and so border on justice ... such as are civility, charity, [and]
liberality."[52] For Locke the rationalist, these are complementary
virtues which only "border on justice"; they have a different basis
and a different function from justice. Beyond a definition of
civility, however, these ideas remain undeveloped. It should also
be noted that for Locke at this point, charity does not include
liberality.

    Locke made one final attempt to construct a unified system
of morality based upon reason. In the Journal entry for

8 February 1677, he refers to the Golden Rule as "that one unquestionable moral rule."[53] This rule, he wrote in another context, is "such a fundamental truth for the regulating (of) human society, that, I think, by that alone, one might without difficulty determine all the cases and doubts in social morality."[54] Unfortunately, Locke was unable to demonstrate the rationality of neighbor-love on the basis of his ethical hedonism. Hence, in *The Reasonableness of Christianity* he turned to revelation for a final vindication of neighbor-love as a universal moral standard and also for a full disclosure of our moral duties here upon earth.[55] While reason is unable to establish neighbor-love as a universal rule, it is able to acknowledge its rationality since it has been made known through revelation. In light of the teachings of Jesus and the Apostles, charity takes on fuller meaning than it had in *Two Treatises*. It now includes mutual good-will, affection, generosity, and self-denial.[56]

When it is understood in terms of neighbor-love, charity includes liberality. Liberality leads, in turn, to a fuller understanding and appreciation of property.[57] To overcome the tendencies toward covetousness and greed, which are "the root of all evil," children should be taught at an early age to be generous with "their friends."[58] The best way to help children "understand property," as well as honesty and justice, "is to lay the foundations of it early in liberality, and an easiness to part with to others whatever they have, or like, themselves." The fullest enjoyment of property, he suggests, is conditioned upon an underlying spirit of liberality, that is, a readiness to give freely and generously to others.[59]

TRUST

Finally, attention needs to be given to the place of trust in Locke's understanding of justice.[60] Trust is "the bond of society." It is the basis upon which society is built. It is also the tie which holds the community together. While Locke develops this idea most fully in terms of the institution and authority of government, it is also implicit in the original compact to form a political society. "Some trust one in another" was already present in the state of nature;

and it was this which made it possible for men to leave that condition and entrust their mutual peace and security to society and ultimately to such government as the community might establish [II.107].

This kind of trust was possible, Laslett proposes, only on the basis of an underlying "natural political virtue."[61] This included such qualities as the following: a sense of common humanity, fidelity, and acknowledgment that oaths, promises, and agreements ought to be kept. It was the presence of these virtues in the state of nature which made it both possible and reasonable for all to turn over their individual executive power to the community as a whole. Once this power has been given to the community, it remains there as long as society endures. For it to do otherwise would be contrary to the original compact itself since no commonwealth can exist without this power [II.243].

Similarly, when the community in turn establishes a government, it does so on the basis of a trust relationship between the rulers and those who are ruled. Magistrates are granted "a fiduciary power" to govern on behalf of the people [II.149]. By the same token, such power is limited by the "express or tacit trust" that it will be used for the good of the people and the preservation of their property [II.149, 171]. The trust itself is forfeited if it is betrayed, and this power reverts to the community, which is now free to establish another government. For Locke, the community always retains "a supreme power" over its rulers; hence, it is able to remove or change them if they betray their trust.

It is the notion of trust which distinguishes Locke's concept of government most sharply from contractual conceptions. For Locke, trust includes at least three basic elements. Firstly, it implies the responsibility on the part of magistrates to serve the public good. Secondly, it presupposes a structure of objective rights which constitute the criteria of positive law. Thirdly, the notion of trust includes the idea of the ultimate accountability of magistrates to the people. Rulers are held accountable for the safeguarding of the public good and the security of their subjects' property. Moreover, the criteria for the public good are defined primarily in terms of certain basic duties and rights based upon the law of nature.[62] It is the people – the community – who decide when a breach of trust has been committed, for only those who depute power can judge whether it has been abused [II.240]. If such controversies cannot be settled peacefully, final appeal is made to God in the form of revolution [II.241].

CHAPTER 6

The American Republic – a case study: civic virtue and the public good

THE IDEOLOGICAL ROOTS OF THE REPUBLIC

Historians and political philosophers differ widely concerning the influence of John Locke upon the Revolutionary generation in America. Although Locke was often cited in support of theories of a social compact, limited government, religious toleration, and natural rights, these ideas had already become deeply embedded in the colonial consciousness as a product of its own distinctive political and religious history.[1] That history included their experience under English domination, their involvement in colonial government, and a long legacy of political resistance and religious dissent reaching back through the Civil War and the Commonwealth (1649–1660) to the Magna Carta in 1215. Their understanding and response to these events was informed, in turn, by a variety of broader intellectual movements which contributed to the development of their own political and religious ideas generally and to their understanding of justice in particular. These ideological traditions were rooted not only in their common English heritage but more broadly and deeply still in the Enlightenment and in medieval and classical thought. Based upon the writings and speeches of the colonial and revolutionary periods, the most influential of these traditions included English common law, the Enlightenment, radical "opposition" – or "country" – political tracts, classical republican virtue, and Puritanism, especially in the form of covenant theology.[2]

It is extremely difficult to assess the relative importance of each of these broader patterns of ideas in the shaping of early American political thought, for none of these traditions existed in isolation from the rest. Fortunately, for purposes of the present study, it is not necessary to enter into this unresolved debate. Our concern is with the diversity and interaction of these differing social, political, and religious forces as they came to bear upon the problem of justice in the Revolutionary and post-Revolutionary periods. Each of these traditions was shaped through interaction with alternative and competing systems of ideas. This process continued both in England and in America. As noted above, covenant theology was influenced by Enlightenment rationalism; and the Puritan divines themselves spoke interchangeably of "the laws of God" and "the laws of nature." Bailyn comments similarly upon the synthesizing as well as the popularizing role of radical social and political ideas represented, both in England and in the colonies, by Opposition political thought, revolutionary tracts, coffee house politicians, and pamphleteers.[3] This legacy of radical thought was informed, he suggests, by ideas drawn from many different sources. Republican virtue also entered the political debate in much the same way. As Gordon S. Wood and J. G. A. Pocock make clear, the idea of virtue as a mutual commitment of the citizenry as a whole to the public good provided a strong counter-force to the atomistic individualism which was often associated with Locke and the Enlightenment.[4] Pocock speaks in this connection of republican virtue as one among a "plurality of languages," or paradigms, which were interacting with each other in the Revolutionary period.[5]

Considered from one perspective, covenant theology – also known as federal theology – was, as Bailyn suggests, "the most limited and parochial" of all of the competing traditions. Viewed from another perspective, however, it "contained the broadest ideas of all," for it provided a theocentric context for the understanding of the events of human history. It also carried belief in the divinely appointed destiny of the colonies (and ultimately of the new Republic) into the eighteenth century and the minds of the Revolutionary generation.[6] This idea, as we shall see, had profound implications for the understanding of justice. While this particular form of theology was confined largely to the colonies in New England, it shared a deep theological kinship with the essentially Calvinist sects in the middle colonies and the Piedmont region of the South. Both were rooted in the Reformed tradition; as such they held similar doctrines of Creation, the sovereignty of God, a divinely established moral order, and human sinfulness.

In the present chapter attention will be focused upon the idea of justice which came to expression in American constitutional thought at the end of the eighteenth century. While this concept was shaped by many different and frequently conflicting moral traditions, it will be argued that the biblical and Puritan covenantal paradigms of community and the righteousness of God provided the basic structure of the idea of justice. It will be argued, additionally, that the religious and theological tradition upon which this idea of justice rested also contributed in distinctive ways to the substantive content of justice through the notions of human dignity, equality, religious liberty, and human rights. Finally, within the context of the religious and moral pluralism of the new Republic, the covenant tradition provided – and still provides – a living source for the transformation of all historical forms of justice, and renewed commitment to the pursuit of justice in the earthly city.

COVENANT AND COMPACT IN COLONIAL AMERICA

The development of American constitutionalism cannot be adequately understood in isolation from its foundations in colonial history. That history included both the moral traditions which we have just noted and the particular institutional forms – compacts, covenants, charters, and "fundamentals" – which were rooted in those traditions.[7] Indeed, so integral was the relationship between the two that the colonists included enumerations of their basic values and commitments in their foundational documents themselves. Typical examples of such listings were the following: The New Haven Fundamentals (1639), the Massachusetts Body of Liberties (1641), the General Laws and Liberties of New Hampshire (1650), Penn's Charter of Liberties (1682), and the New York Charter of Liberties and Privileges (1683). These charters and fundamentals provided the basis for what later came to be called bills of rights.[8] The basic values contained in these documents constituted the "self-definition" element in the founding documents.[9] They defined both the moral basis and the moral identity – or character – of the newly created political bodies. The values and commitments themselves were rooted in turn in much older traditions running back to the Protestant Reformation and the Bible, to classical ideas of virtue and natural law, and to English common law.

In order to obtain a clearer understanding of the moral foundations of the new Republic, we turn first to the covenant form of community in the New England colonies. What is the relationship between ecclesiastical and civil covenants? How were covenants related to compacts? Finally, in what respects do covenants and compacts differ from contracts? With this background in view, we will then be in a position to inquire whether – and in what ways – the American Republic was conceived from its beginning as a covenant people. If it was so conceived, what were the implications of this understanding for law and justice in the context of the religious and cultural pluralism of the new nation?

It has been previously noted (chapter four) that for the Puritans all forms of community are fundamentally covenantal. All persons, they believed, are endowed with natural liberty; at the same time all are subject to the universal law of nature.[10] Since this law is written on the heart, it is discernible by reason; it is also revealed in Scripture. It includes not only the basic principles of justice but also those virtues which are essential to such human relationships as friendship, community, and social order. Nature similarly teaches that humanity should join together in social covenants and "dwell together in Societies." What nature teaches in this regard is likewise confirmed by revelation. In terms that anticipated Locke's "social compact" the Puritans also viewed humankind as leaving a state of nature – a state of natural liberty and law of nature – and entering a social state based upon a mutually binding covenant.

In addition to the common destiny of all people to live together in societies, the Puritans believed that God had established a special covenant with them as his elect. He had chosen them to be a "new Israel," a "city upon a hill," a model of Christ's kingdom upon earth.[11] Accordingly, when they formed new communities, they entered into a covenant with God and also with one another to be God's people and to obey his law. On the basis of this primary commitment they formed two other covenants – one political and the other ecclesiastical – for the institutional ordering of their common life.

The Mayflower Compact (1620) is the most familiar and perhaps the earliest covenant in colonial America.[12] Though it contains only three brief paragraphs, it includes both a social and a political covenant. After first calling upon God as witness, the signatories of the document set forth their purposes in coming to the new land: "for the glorie of God, and advancements of the Christian faith and honour of our king and countrie." They then "solemnly & mutualy ... covenant and combine [themselves] togeather into a civil body politick" for the "better ordering, & preservation & furtherance" of those ends. Having thus bound themselves together in a civil society they promise to enact such laws and establish such forms of government as are deemed "most meete & convenient for the generall good of the Colonie." The political covenant ends with the "promise [of] all due submission and obedience" to such laws and civil authorities. Other examples of communities formed on the basis of a social covenant include Salem (the Salem Covenant, 1629); Massachusetts Bay (1630); Plymouth (the Pilgrim Code of Law, 1636); and Eastchester (the Ten Farms Covenant, 1665).

For a fuller exposition of the covenantal model of Puritan society we turn once more to Winthrop's sermon, "A Model of Christian Charity."[13] In that masterful discourse delivered en route to New England in 1630, Winthrop describes the kind of community which he and his companions had been commissioned to establish at Massachusetts Bay. The work in which they are engaged, he notes, is "by a mutual consent." Winthrop then sets forth the purpose of their journey: "to seek out a place of cohabitation and consortship, under a due form of government both civil and ecclesiastical." In this endeavor "the care of the public" must overrule all private concerns. Underlying the civil and ecclesiastical forms of government which they are about to establish, he continues, is the fundamental covenant whereby God has chosen them to be "His own people": "Thus stands the cause between God and us: we are entered into covenant with Him for this work; we have taken out a commission, the Lord hath given us leave to draw our own articles." If they are brought safely to their destination, this will be a sign that this covenant has been "ratified" and their commission sealed by an overruling Providence. They are to be "a city upon a hill"; the eyes of all the people will be upon them. If they are faithful to the covenant, they will be blessed; but if they are disobedient to the command-ments of God and to the articles of their covenant with him, they will be destroyed.

The Mayflower Compact and covenant described by Win-throp are typical of numerous founding documents in colonial America.[14] The terms "covenant" and "compact" were used interchangeably during this period. While political covenants were modelled more directly after church covenants and invoked God as witness, compacts included secularized agreements as well. Some documents which were essentially covenants were also called compacts. Thus, for example, the "Mayflower Compact," originally known informally among the settlers as "The Plymouth Combination," was first given its present title by a historian who published it in 1793; in reality, it is also a covenant. Most importantly, for present purposes, both cove-nants and compacts were binding agreements based upon mutual consent, and both created political communities. Both included explanations about why the agreement was needed. Both created a "people" and a government; and both defined the kind of people the new body wished to become. Sometimes these agreements also contained a constitution, which provided for the creation of particular political instruments for decision-making and governance. In such cases the covenant/compact constituted a complete founding document.[15] In other instances, however, the constitution comprised a separate document which was added later to the initial covenant/compact; together the two formed a founding instrument.

When the Americans created state constitutions during the Revolutionary Period, they drew together elements from the various kinds of documents which were familiar to them from their colonial experience reaching back to 1620. These included covenants, compacts, charters, frames, fundamentals, and ordinances. Ideas and forms contained in these materials had been developed and woven together in the course of the seventeenth and eighteenth centuries. In this way they entered into the creation not only of state constitutions but also of the national Constitution of 1787. Covenants and compacts had provided the basis not only for the formation of separate political communities, but also for their joining together in a variety of associations and "confederations" based upon a federal model of government. The Fundamental Orders of Connecticut (1639) and the New England Confederation (1643) are typical examples of such organizations. Since the distinction between confederalism and federalism had not been clearly drawn at that time, the colonists used the term "confederation" to refer to what today would be called federations. In such confederations the identity and control of the local bodies was maintained along with an agreement to subordinate their own governmental power to that of a central authority in certain specified areas of concern such as mutual defense. Both terms refer to a dual – a local and a regional – rather than an unitary system of government. For the Puritans, a model for such alliances was found in the ancient confederacy of Israelite tribes.

In sum, both the covenant and the compact images of society were strongly communal. In this respect they contrasted sharply with contractarian concepts of social origins, which tended to be more atomistic, more legalistic, and more provisional or conditional. Compared with the latter, covenants and compacts were based upon profoundly different conceptions of human nature, community, and the moral order underlying human history. In addition to liberty, equality, and human rights, both stressed the primacy of the public good. While these ideas underwent profound changes in the course of the seventeenth and eighteenth centuries, they helped define the moral basis of the new Republic and the kind of "people" the Founders wanted it to become. Covenant theology helped to provide a distinctive understanding of the new Republic based upon a particular theological tradition, rooted in the Calvinist wing of the Reformation and more basically still in Scripture.

THE CREATION OF THE REPUBLIC (1776–1787)

In the decade between the Declaration of Independence and the ratification of the national Constitution the new states were faced with the necessity of forming some kind of union, firstly, to provide mutual support in the achievement of independence and, secondly, to create a national government for the pursuit of mutual ends. Lutz suggests that in this process they entered into a national covenant, or compact, represented by two founding documents.[16] The Declaration of Independence came first: it created a people and set forth the basic values, rights, and commitments underlying the struggle against oppression and tyranny. The Constitution of 1787 comprised the second part of the national compact. Through it "the people," which had already been brought into being through the Declaration, established a particular form of government. Through it they made provision for voter eligibility, representation, and the holding of public office; they also determined the powers and limits of those governmental bodies created by the Constitution. Significantly, they also provided for the amendment of that basic document itself.

Both the Declaration and the Constitution, Lutz notes, are foundational; together with the Bill of Rights (ratified as part of the Constitution in 1791), they comprise the American constitutional system as it stands today.[17] Unlike the Constitution, which does not make any religious claims, the Declaration appeals directly to "the Laws of Nature and of Nature's God" as the basis of the claim to independence. It also includes an appeal to "the Supreme Judge of the world" and a commitment to reliance upon "divine Providence." Viewed together, the Declaration thus provides "a continuing link between our national compact and the covenant tradition from which it is derived."[18]

AN EXPERIMENT IN REPRESENTATIVE DEMOCRACY

The Constitution was a compact or a secular covenant. Unlike earlier compacts between the people and their rulers it was a compact among the people themselves: the rulers and the people had become one.[19] The new republic was an experiment in democracy; more precisely, it was an experiment in representative democracy. The people governed, but they did so indirectly through elected representatives rather than directly through personal participation in decision-making.

Representation – "the delegation of the government ... to a small number of citizens elected by the rest" (Madison) – was the key to understanding the uniqueness of the American system of governance. The fundamentally new idea in this experiment, Gordon Wood suggests, was the belief that power resides in the people, who delegate this power to representatives to be used for the public good, and that the representatives, in turn, should be held accountable to the people for their stewardship.[20] Governance by the people, delegation of power, the primacy of the public good, and accountability of elected representatives – these were the key elements in the republic which the Founders envisioned.

The Republican ideal

While representation was the key to the *uniqueness* of the American experiment, the most fundamental idea of all was the belief that the people have an inalienable right to rule themselves. This was the underlying reason for the colonists' revolt against the Crown. In the place of colonial dependence and monarchical rule, they undertook to establish a free and independent federation based upon the sovereignty of the people. In so doing, however, they were confronted with a profound paradox in the republican ideal. Republicanism is committed to the belief that the primary purpose of the state is to promote the public good and that a republic is best-suited to that end. Since in such a state the people govern themselves, a republic is uniquely dependent upon virtue and most especially upon the commitment of the citizens to the public good (civic virtue).[21] It is precisely at this point, however, that republicanism is confronted with its most critical challenge: how can a state which is based upon popular virtue safeguard itself against internal corruption and decay?

The problem itself had been the subject of continuing debate running back through English history and the Enlightenment to the Renaissance and ultimately to classical political thought, including Aristotle's description of the *polis*. During the period of the Italian Renaissance, the Florentine Republic (early sixteenth century) came to be viewed as a paradigmatic example of a state founded upon the republican principle of democratic rule. In the controversies which ensued regarding the durability and ultimate fate of the republic, Machiavelli argued that civic virtue alone could not sustain it against the threat of "fortune" and "corruption."[22] In time virtue would be destroyed by ambition, greed, and factionalism. Machiavelli recommended "audacity" (*virtù*) in the face of fortune. By "audacity" he meant the ability to dominate or control fortune. Understood in this sense, *virtù* had a strongly military quality; hence, he advocated a citizen militia. Military training and discipline, he believed, would increase the *virtù* of the people and enhance their sense of patriotism and devotion to the state. While such a strategy would not prevent the final dissolution of the republic, it provided the most effective means of perpetuating its existence through time.

The legacy of republicanism and the controversies surrounding it were transmitted through the Renaissance and the Enlightenment to England and America in the seventeenth and eighteenth centuries. There it became an important element in the political debates about resistance to arbitrary government, liberty, and human rights. In itself, the republican ideal confronted the framers of the American Constitution with the same dilemma which had been faced by the Florentines in the sixteenth century, namely, the problem of how a republic could flourish and endure. In the words of Pocock, this was their "Machiavellian moment" – the moment when they faced the ambiguity and precariousness of their experiment in democratic governance.[23]

Popular sovereignty rests upon three basic assumptions.[24] The first and most fundamental of these is the belief that the people are virtuous – that they are able and willing to place the public good above private interest. The other two are derivative; as such, they represent implications and qualifications of the first. Accordingly, the second underlying principle is the belief that, if they are informed and if they are given sufficient time for deliberation, the people can distinguish between what is for the public good and what is not. Since the people individually often do not have either the requisite time or the necessary information, one of the functions of representative democracy is to make provision for both through the electoral process. Moreover, it was assumed that elections would result in the selection of persons of superior virtue as well as ability. The representatives would then help to educate and lead the people through the electoral process. If in practice representative government contained an inherent aristocratic principle, it was designed to secure the public good more effectively than direct democracy; such government was still democratic since the representatives were ultimately accountable to the people. The third assumption underlying popular government is the belief that the people acting together as a common body have a disposition to choose the public good over their own private interests. In contrast, persons acting separately as single individuals are more likely to pursue their own private welfare.

Threats of corruption and tyranny

In debates surrounding the formation of the national Constitution, both Federalists and Anti-federalists advocated popular government in its republican form.[25] The differences between them pertained to the types of republican society which they sought and the particular form of federal system which was best-suited to that end. The Anti-federalists envisioned a social order which closely resembled the classical ideal of a small, pastoral republic composed of virtuous, self-reliant citizens who managed their own affairs and shunned the lures of commerce and empire.[26] They believed that small, localized government provides the strongest protection against corruption and tyranny because it is most directly controlled by the people. Small states foster close relationships between elected officials and the people; they create a community of shared habits and values, and they also tend to prevent great disparities of wealth. In short, they nurture close associational ties, the cultivation of virtue, and relationships of trust and accountability between the citizenry and their representatives. For all these reasons Anti-federalists tended to oppose the national Constitution in its original form and argued instead for a confederacy of small republics in which government was directly controlled by the people.

Constitutional protections

If the Anti-federalists believed that the greatest threat to the Republic lay in a strong centralized government, what the Federalists such as Madison feared most was factionalism. Factions arise whenever a portion of the citizens – either a minority or the majority – unite around a passion or interest which is contrary either to individual rights or to the public good. Factions represent the threat of two different forms of tyranny. Madison was primarily concerned with the danger posed by majorities since minorities would be amenable to democratic control by majority vote. In order to protect both minorities and the people as a whole against tyranny imposed by the majority, other safeguards are needed. To provide such protections Federalists advocated separation of powers among the legislative, executive, and judicial branches of government, and a series of checks and balances within the constitutional system itself.[27] The purpose of such stipulations, it should be noted, was not to circumvent popular rule but, to enhance the latter by providing time for deliberation and preventing the domination of any particular faction.

In its final form the national Constitution represented a series of compromises and built-in tensions. Examples of these include – but are not limited to – the following. Firstly, it created a mixed form of government. The Republic was a representative democracy. In this respect it differed sharply from a pure democracy in which the people participate directly in their own governance, as in a town meeting. Viewed from one perspective, the national government embodies not only the democratic principle (the lower house) but also the aristocratic (upper house) and monarchic (executive) principles, all held in check through a separation of powers and a series of checks and balances. Secondly, dual citizenship – state and national – was recognized. At the same time provision was made for the division of powers between state and national governments.[28] Thirdly, to provide further protection against factions, Madison argued for an "extended republic." He believed that because of their geographic size, greater populations, and diversity, large republics constitute a stronger safeguard against the tyranny of minorities than do smaller societies. From a Federalist perspective, therefore, provisions for the ratification of the Constitution by nine states and the admission of new states were "republican remedies" for the disease of factionalism.[29] Fourthly, at the insistence of the Anti-federalists a Bill of Rights (1789) was subsequently added to the 1787 Constitution to provide further protection against encroachment of government upon basic liberties and rights.

Two additional features of the Constitution are particularly important in this regard. First, provision is made for the amendment of the Constitution itself (Article V). Such amendments may be proposed either by Congress or by a Constitutional Convention, and they must be ratified by the legislatures of three-fourths of the states or by conventions in the same number of states. Wood calls this provision for reform "a healing principle."[30] It allows for future improvement and change by the people through peaceful means. In this sense it is the quintessential expression of the republican principle of the sovereignty of the people.

Secondly, the First Amendment of the Constitution provides that "Congress shall make no law respecting an establishment of religion, or prohibiting the free exercise thereof ..."[31] This Amendment contains two important provisions governing church-state relations at the national level. On the one hand, it prohibits the establishment of any form of religion; and on the other it protects "the free exercise" of religion. Both of these principles – and also the proper relationship between them – have been interpreted in a variety of ways in the course of American history. Although the debates have often been framed in terms of separation of church and state, Katz argues that the fundamental American principle of church-state relations is religious liberty.[32] Such liberty, he continues, is "incompatible with an absolute separation of church and state." The only form of separation which the Constitution requires is that "which promotes religious liberty." Thus, while the non-establishment clause requires the and national governments.[28] Thirdly, to provide further protection against factions, Madison argued for an "extended republic." He believed that because of their geographic size, greater populations, and diversity, large republics constitute a stronger safeguard against the tyranny of minorities than do smaller societies. From a Federalist perspective, therefore, provisions for the ratification of the Constitution by nine states and the admission of new states were "republican remedies" for the disease of factionalism.[29] Fourthly, at the insistence of the Anti-federalists a Bill of Rights (1789) was subsequently added to the 1787 Constitution to provide further protection against encroachment of government upon basic liberties and rights.

Two additional features of the Constitution are particularly important in this regard. First, provision is made for the amendment of the Constitution itself (Article V). Such amendments may be proposed either by Congress or by a Constitutional Convention, and they must be ratified by the legislatures of three-fourths of the states or by conventions in the same number of states. Wood calls this provision for reform "a healing principle."[30] It allows for future improvement and change by the people through peaceful means. In this sense it is the quintessential expression of the republican principle of the sovereignty of the people.

Secondly, the First Amendment of the Constitution provides that "Congress shall make no law respecting an establishment of religion, or prohibiting the free exercise thereof …"[31] This Amendment contains two important provisions governing church-state relations at the national level. On the one hand, it prohibits the establishment of any form of religion; and on the other it protects "the free exercise" of religion. Both of these principles – and also the proper relationship between them – have been interpreted in a variety of ways in the course of American history. Although the debates have often been framed in terms of separation of church and state, Katz argues that the fundamental American principle of church-state relations is religious liberty.[32] Such liberty, he continues, is "incompatible with an absolute separation of church and state." The only form of separation which the Constitution requires is that "which promotes religious liberty." Thus, while the non-establishment clause requires the

running back through English history and the Enlightenment to the Renaissance and ultimately to classical political thought, including Aristotle's description of the *polis*. During the period of the Italian Renaissance, the Florentine Republic (early sixteenth century) came to be viewed as a paradigmatic example of a state founded upon the republican principle of democratic rule. In the controversies which ensued regarding the durability and ultimate fate of the republic, Machiavelli argued that civic virtue alone could not sustain it against the threat of "fortune" and "corruption."[22] In time virtue would be destroyed by ambition, greed, and factionalism. Machiavelli recommended "audacity" (*virtù*) in the face of fortune. By "audacity" he meant the ability to dominate or control fortune. Understood in this sense, *virtù* had a strongly military quality; hence, he advocated a citizen militia. Military training and discipline, he believed, would increase the *virtù* of the people and enhance their sense of patriotism and devotion to the state. While such a strategy would not prevent the final dissolution of the republic, it provided the most effective means of perpetuating its existence through time.

The legacy of republicanism and the controversies surrounding it were transmitted through the Renaissance and the Enlightenment to England and America in the seventeenth and eighteenth centuries. There it became an important element in the political debates about resistance to arbitrary government, liberty, and human rights. In itself, the republican ideal confronted the framers of the American Constitution with the same dilemma which had been faced by the Florentines in the sixteenth century, namely, the problem of how a republic could flourish and endure. In the words of Pocock, this was their "Machiavellian moment" – the moment when they faced the ambiguity and precariousness of their experiment in democratic governance.[23]

Popular sovereignty rests upon three basic assumptions.[24] The first and most fundamental of these is the belief that the people are virtuous – that they are able and willing to place the public good above private interest. The other two are derivative; as such, they represent implications and qualifications of the first. Accordingly, the second underlying principle is the belief that, if they are informed and if they are given sufficient time for deliberation, the people can distinguish between what is for the public good and what is not. Since the people individually often do not have either the requisite time or the necessary information, one of the functions of representative democracy is to make provision for both through the electoral process. Moreover, it was assumed that elections would result in the selection of persons of superior virtue as well as ability. The representatives would then help to educate and lead the people through the electoral process. If in practice representative government contained an inherent aristocratic principle, it was designed to secure the public good more effectively than direct democracy; such government was still democratic since the representatives were ultimately accountable to the people. The third assumption underlying popular government is the belief that the people acting together as a common body have a disposition to choose the public good over their own private interests. In contrast, persons acting separately as single individuals are more likely to pursue their own private welfare.

Threats of corruption and tyranny

In debates surrounding the formation of the national Constitution, both Federalists and Anti-federalists advocated popular government in its republican form.[25] The differences between them pertained to the types of republican society which they sought and the particular form of federal system which was best-suited to that end. The Anti-federalists envisioned a social order which closely resembled the classical ideal of a small, pastoral republic composed of virtuous, self-reliant citizens who managed their own affairs and shunned the lures of commerce and empire.[26] They believed that small, localized government provides the strongest protection against corruption and tyranny because it is most directly controlled by the people. Small states foster close relationships between elected officials and the people; they create a community of shared habits and values, and they also tend to prevent great disparities of wealth. In short, they nurture close associational ties, the cultivation of virtue, and relationships of trust and accountability between the citizenry and their representatives. For all these reasons Anti-federalists tended

to oppose the national Constitution in its original form and argued instead for a confederacy of small republics in which government was directly controlled by the people.

Constitutional protections

If the Anti-federalists believed that the greatest threat to the Republic lay in a strong centralized government, what the Federalists such as Madison feared most was factionalism. Factions arise whenever a portion of the citizens – either a minority or the majority – unite around a passion or interest which is contrary either to individual rights or to the public good. Factions represent the threat of two different forms of tyranny. Madison was primarily concerned with the danger posed by majorities since minorities would be amenable to democratic control by majority vote. In order to protect both minorities and the people as a whole against tyranny imposed by the majority, other safeguards are needed. To provide such protections Federalists advocated separation of powers among the legislative, executive, and judicial branches of government, and a series of checks and balances within the constitutional system itself.[27] The purpose of such stipulations, it should be noted, was not to circumvent popular rule but, to enhance the latter by providing time for deliberation and preventing the domination of any particular faction.

In its final form the national Constitution represented a series of compromises and built-in tensions. Examples of these include – but are not limited to – the following. Firstly, it created a mixed form of government. The Republic was a representative democracy. In this respect it differed sharply from a pure democracy in which the people participate directly in their own governance, as in a town meeting. Viewed from one perspective, the national government embodies not only the democratic principle (the lower house) but also the aristocratic (upper house) and monarchic (executive) principles, all held in check through a separation of powers and a series of checks and balances. Secondly, dual citizenship – state and national – was recognized. At the same time provision was made for the division of powers between state institutional separation of church and state, it does not require a separation of religion and government. Such a position would have been unthinkable to the Founders and also to the citizenry at large.[33] The primary purpose of the prohibition of the establishment of religion is to protect the free exercise of religion as a basic human right. Institutional separation of church and state at the national level was also necessitated by the religious pluralism of the new Republic and by the fact that different churches were established in different states with the sole exceptions of Rhode Island and Pennsylvania.

LAW, RELIGION, AND THE DEMOCRATIC PROCESS

In the present chapter attention has been focused upon the founding of the American Republic as a case study in the interaction of law and religion. "Despite the tensions between them," Berman has observed, "one cannot flourish without the other."[34] Commenting in a similar vein upon the relationship of religion to American democracy in the first half of the nineteenth century, Tocqueville wrote: "Religion in America takes no direct part in the government of society, but it must nevertheless be regarded as the foremost of the political institutions of that country." Religion "facilitates the use of free institutions," he continued; moreover, Americans generally hold religion to be "indispensable to the maintenance of republican institutions."[35]

In order to understand the role of religion in the shaping of American political thought in the revolutionary period, it has been necessary to consider a number of other ideological influences and traditions. None of these forces operated independently of the others. It was through their mutual interaction that each contributed to the shaping of the political process, and to the development of the American constitutional system. Particular attention has been given to the nature and basis of human society, whether in covenant or compact or contract. Special attention has also been given to republican – or civic – virtue, which was generally assumed to be necessary both for the flourishing of the republic and for its survival through time. Beneath this consensus, however, there were deep differences not only about the possibilities and limits of virtue but also about the nature and springs of the latter.

Pocock called this point at which the Founders of the American Republic confronted the paradox of both the necessity and the fragility of virtue their "Machiavellian moment."[36] While they wrestled with this paradox, they never fully resolved it. It is not surprising, therefore, that the polarities and tensions between the underlying political philosophies are reflected in the Constitution itself. Indeed, both Federalists and Anti-Federalists supported the final document and sought its ratification by the states precisely because such polarities and tensions are there. Examples of such conflicts include the system of checks and balances, the relationship between the states and the national government, the process of amendment, and separation of church and state. As such these tensions are continuing sources of strength and vitality in American democracy. Now as then, the Republic is still an experiment in democratic governance, "testing whether this nation or any nation so conceived and so dedicated can long endure."[37]

CHAPTER 7

Covenant, justice, and law

THE COVENANTAL BASIS OF SOCIETY

The polarities and tensions reflected in the debates surrounding the creation of the American republic were rooted in fundamentally different presuppositions – about the moral ordering of history, the dignity and goodness of human nature, and the basis and proper end of civil society. The purpose in choosing the founding of the American republic as a case study was to use that event as an illustration of the way in which one particular theological tradition approached the problems of justice and law during the formative years of the new nation. During that time a distinctively new form of government was established whereby the people rule themselves under a system of laws which they have made and to which they have given their assent.

In that process the Puritan – and ultimately biblical – idea of covenant provided the most fundamental symbol for understanding both the basis of society and the nature of the Founders' own undertaking. "It is of the nature and essence of every society," Winthrop had noted, "to be knit together by some covenant, either expressed or implied."[1] The adoption of this paradigm did not issue in the establishment of Puritanism. Rather, it signified the unity of a people knit together by mutual commitment to each other in a common endeavor, a commitment based finally upon promise and trust.

Not only did covenant serve as the mediator of an essentially biblical and communal conception of society; it also provided the basis for a synthesis of reason and revelation grounded in a strong doctrine of Creation. The Puritan notion of the covenantal basis of society, it will be recalled, rested ultimately upon the covenant of works which God established with Adam and through Adam with all humanity in Creation. Unlike the covenant of grace, which was limited to the elect, the covenant of works provided a theological basis for moral, civil, and religious obligations based upon the law of the nature which was given in Creation.[2]

Standing as it did in the Reformed tradition, Puritanism held that God reveals himself both through nature and through Scripture. While there is no contradiction between the two forms of knowledge, the distinctiveness and primacy of Scripture is maintained. It should be noted in this connection that Roman Catholicism also provides a similar synthesis of the two through its doctrine of "natural law." Since the colonists were predominantly Protestant, however, the natural law tradition was transmitted to America primarily in secularized form through the Enlightenment.

In a pluralistic and increasingly secular society, covenant meant a commitment to religious liberty and diversity. It meant institutional separation of church and state; but is also meant the free exercise of religion. The prohibition of an established church at the national level was not due, of course, to Puritanism itself but to necessity. Puritanism was the official form of religion in all of the New England colonies save Rhode Island. Among Protestants only Quakers and Baptists opposed establishment on principle. In addition, free thinkers such as the Deists were likewise opposed on principle. Thus, while Puritanism was established at the state level in New England, at the national level covenant presupposed commitment to a secular state in which different religious groups are free not only to worship as they choose but also to participate in the political process according to the guidance of conscience.

VIRTUE, COVENANT, AND PLURALISM

In the course of our study it has been argued that the concept of justice as virtue needs to be supplemented by a concept of law which not only includes but also transcends positive law. At the same time it has also been argued that while justice includes law, justice is not finally reducible to law. Covenant points to the fundamental unity of virtue and law in a concept of community and, more especially, of political community based upon mutual trust and fidelity to a common cause.

For the Puritans, this cause was the building of "a city upon a hill," a civil community modelled after the kingdom of God.[3] Stated in the broader, more secular terms of the Revolutionary generation in America, delegates to the Continental Congress in 1776–1777 joined in declaring their independence and in the mutual pledging of their lives, their fortunes, and their honor to the attainment of that end. It is unclear whether the Declaration of Independence was intended fundamentally as an agreement among the several states, thus representing thirteen different peoples, or as a document which created a single people at the national level.[4] In any event, through it the colonists were united in a common enterprise and in their pledge of mutual fidelity to each other in the pursuit of that goal. Similarly, the Constitution of 1787 presupposed the existence of a single people bound together by a common purpose. That purpose included the formation of "a more perfect union" than that which had existed thus far under the Articles of Confederation, the establishment of justice, provision for the common defense, assurance of domestic peace, promotion of the general welfare, and the securing of the blessings of liberty both to that generation and to their posterity.[5] As noted above, taken together the Declaration and the federal Constitution constitute a national covenant/compact based upon a covenantal understanding of political community. This covenant was a mutual commitment of the people to be bound together under the rule of law to promote justice and peace.

For MacIntyre the possibility of justice is limited to societies whose members share a common narrative and seek a common goal. In *After Virtue* his analysis of justice rests upon an elitist and sectarian conception of community and morality which fails to take sufficient account of the resources which pluralism provides for the enrichment of community and a fuller understanding of justice. When he defines human action as action for which someone is accountable, accountability means intelligibility in terms of a shared narrative.[6] Morality is interpreted basically in teleological terms. The recovery of justice depends upon the development of new forms of community based upon a shared tradition of virtue and a common goal. Although the idea of covenant has often been employed in an exclusivist manner, in its biblical roots it provides the basis for a broader conception of human community, a greater affirmation of pluralism, and a more dynamic concept of justice than are found in the tradition of virtue.[7] It points to the inseparability of justice as an internal disposition and justice as external deeds; it points both to justice as law and to a transcendent norm by which all systems of human justice are measured and finally judged.

COVENANT, RESPONSIBILITY, AND ACCOUNTABILITY

The basic meaning of covenant can be made clearer by reference to H. Richard Niebuhr's concept of "responsibility." Niebuhr uses this symbol to define the fundamental structure of moral relationships in terms of the responses of the self in an ongoing moral community rather than in terms of aspiration after an ideal good (teleology) or obedience to abstract duties or absolute laws (deontology).[8] Two aspects of "responsibility" are particularly relevant to our attempt to understand the nature and meaning of justice from a covenantal perspective. Attention will be given both to the underlying conception of moral agency and to Niebuhr's relational theory of value and moral norms.

For Niebuhr, ethics begins with reflection upon *"that which is."*[9] Stated in theological terms, the primary question of ethics is "What is God doing?" The ethics of responsibility affirms: "God is acting in all actions upon you. So respond to all actions upon you as to respond to his action."[10] The question concerning the divine action is primary for Niebuhr because it places human action in the context of its ultimate dependence upon the sovereignty of God in human history. For Niebuhr, God is active in all events and all relationships as Creator, as Orderer and Judge, and as the Redeemer (Reconciler) of all creation to himself. Human action is action done in response to this three-fold pattern of divine action; it is at the same time action in response to the action of other selves in a moral community that is ultimately universal. Niebuhr's ethics is strongly theocentric. It is also based upon a covenantal understanding of God's relationship to the world and a covenantal understanding of community. The self thus conceived is essentially social: it comes into being and continues in existence through its relationships with other selves. Viewed from this perspective, moral agency is most adequately understood as the response of the self to the action of other selves (individuals and groups) in the context of ultimate dependence upon the moral ordering of history. The freedom of the self is limited not only by the action of other humans but, more fundamentally, by the divine action.

For Niebuhr, divine action and human freedom are inseparably bound together in moral experience. It is sometimes suggested that the symbol of the self-as-responder represents an excessively passive conception of moral agency.[11] From Niebuhr's perspective, however, the teleological image of the self-as-maker acting in pursuit of some end fails to give adequate attention to the conditioned character of all human action. As the primary metaphor of morality it implies too large a scope for human autonomy in the pursuit of ideal goals and ends. At the same time the deontological image of the self-as-citizen living under law fails to give adequate attention to the role of the self in the determination of its action. Viewed in terms of obligation and duty, freedom is limited to the freedom to be obedient to some law, whether it be the law of reason or the divine law. In contrast to both of the foregoing images of moral agency, in an ethics of responsibility freedom means the freedom to respond, first of all, to the divine action and, secondly, to the action of other selves and to the events of nature.

Thus understood freedom is not a static or fixed capacity of the self. On the contrary, it is a dynamic, relational reality. Human freedom refers to those actions which are subject, in some degree, to human influence and control. Theologically, the dimensions of freedom must always be understood in terms of the experience of the Christian community as part of the human community "in time and history."[12] The dimensions and meaning of freedom are shaped not only by historical events and circumstances but also by their interpretation by the agent, and by the agent's understanding of its own past and future action. The symbol of "response" is open-ended to the discovery of newer horizons of freedom than Niebuhr himself perceived, but if the question of human action replaced that of the divine action as the starting point of ethical reflection, the symbol itself would be transformed into teleology.

For Niebuhr the metaphor of responsibility does not so much replace the other images of moral agency, as it supplements and reinterprets the latter. All three symbols are needed; each contributes to our understanding of the multiple dimensions of moral action. The same is also true of the corresponding conceptions of moral norms. In teleological ethics the moral norm is defined in terms of the *good* (ends and values). In deontological ethics it is defined in terms of the *right* (conformity to rules and law). In contrast, in an ethics of responsibility the moral norm is understood in terms of the *fitting* (or appropriate) action.[13] Here again all three images are needed for a fuller understanding of moral relationships. The fitting response includes elements of the good and the right; in this context, however, these are reinterpreted in relational terms.

As noted above, Niebuhr's concept of moral agency is integrally related to his relational concept of value. Here, again, ethical reflection begins with "that which is" rather than with idealistic or abstract conceptions of "the good" and "the right." Interpreted in relational terms, value does not exist independently; it is, rather, a function of being-in-relation to other beings. Value arises out of the capacities, the needs, and the potentialities of beings in their interrelationships with each other. In teleological ethics moral norms are defined in terms of goods; in deontological ethics, they are understood in terms of duty. In an ethics of responsibility, they are understood in terms of the *fitting* or the *appropriate* action or response. Here, "the good" and "the right" refer to action which best fulfills the potentialities, meets the needs, or corresponds to the capacities of the neighbor.[14] Since they are grounded ontologically in the relationship of being-to-being, moral norms are objective. As such they are relational without being psychologically relativistic. Understood in terms of responsibility, the human task is to decide what particular actions are most fitting or most appropriate under particular historical circumstances. Such decisions require a capacity for moral discernment – an ability to perceive and interpret the complexity and ambiguity of moral choices and a capacity for discrimination among the competing goods and duties.[15] In theocentric ethics, discernment includes the capacity to perceive and interpret the fundamental patterns of God's relationship to the world and a readiness to respond to the divine action within the context of the community of faith.

While Niebuhr developed the meaning of responsibility primarily in terms of the individual moral agent, there is nevertheless implicit in the idea the basis for a concept of justice as a task for the community. At the formal level Niebuhr defined responsibility as a pattern of response to prior action, interpretation of that prior action, accountability of the self for its response, and participation in an ongoing moral community.[16] At a less abstract level, however, the meaning of responsibility was expressed concretely and collectively in the history of Israel as a covenant people.[17] Among the Israelites all human relationships were fundamentally covenantal. They were based upon the making and keeping of promises. Domestic, economic, and political relations, as well as religious observances, were essentially covenantal relations among persons based upon the covenant between God and humanity. Such an understanding of community contained a place for law, but covenant pointed beyond the law to the basis of the law in underlying human relationships. Natural, historical, and cultural connections were transformed into covenant bonds without losing their natural basis in history and culture. Niebuhr's description of the family is typical in this regard of all other human relationships: "The family, with all its natural basis in sex and parental love, was now given a sub-foundation as it were in promise and the keeping of faith between husbands and wives, parents and children."

ACCOUNTABILITY AND DEMOCRACY

To interpret human community, including political community, in terms of covenant is to understand it basically in terms of promise and trust.[18] Our humanity is most fully expressed in acts of commitment to each other and in faithfulness to a common cause. Such a pattern of mutual promise and entrustment is not limited, moreover, to those who share the same moral tradition, the same vision, and the same narrative which MacIntyre's account of virtue presupposes. Stated in terms of biblical mono-theism, covenant is rooted in faith in the sovereignty and right-eousness of God. Such faith relativizes the moral claims of all historical communities; at the same time it also affirms the reality of a universal human community grounded in God's creating, ordering, and reconciling relationship to the world. Understood in terms of the divine covenant with humanity, pluralism is part of God's design for the enrichment and ordering of human history. Its inclusion in the political process is prerequisite for the achievement of justice. Pluralism provides the broadest possible resources not only for a fuller insight into the meaning of justice but also for the attainment of justice within the limits of history.

In a covenantal understanding of public life, accountability is the willingness of officials to be held accountable by the people *as a whole.* In America provision for such accountability of elected representatives is an essential and distinctive feature of representative democracy. Power is entrusted by the people to elected representatives to be used for the public good; the representatives, in turn, are held accountable to the people for their stewardship. All of this takes place within the context of a form of government and a set of laws that are determined by the people – rulers and ruled together – as a whole. Both the form of government and the fundamental law are established through the adoption of a constitution. Provision is also made for amending the Constitution and for the enactment of new laws by the legislative branch of government. In the provision for amendments there is implicit recognition of a transcending form or dimension of justice in terms of which the written law can be changed and adapted to new historical circumstances. Not only are elected representatives accountable to the people for the public good; both elected officials and the people are accountable ultimately to God for human justice measured finally by the justice and righteousness of God.

JUSTICE AS OBLIGATION

In its biblical form justice is a duty, or obligation, based upon God's covenant with humanity. The demand for justice is grounded in God's claim upon humankind whom he has created to live in covenantal relationships with himself and with each other. Not only is covenantal justice theocentric; its meaning is defined in terms of obedience to divinely given commandments which are addressed both to individuals and to the people as a whole. The commandments include Israel's duties toward God; they also include duties of the people toward one another.

While the stress falls upon obligation, the biblical idea of justice also contains an implicit notion of *human rights*. Since all persons are made in the "image of God," all are endowed with equal claims to justice. Not only does God require justice for all, he shows special concern for the poor and oppressed because they are most vulnerable and because they have no one to plead their cause in the courts. As we shall see, however, such justice claims differ sharply from modern individualistic conceptions of natural rights. Whereas the former are derived primarily from covenant-obligations of the community as a whole, the latter represent claims which are inherent in autonomous individuals. Biblical justice includes both duties and "rights": both the duty of those in positions of power to do justice and the corresponding claim – or "right" – of all to be treated justly.

According to traditional Christian teaching from New Testament times down to the Protestant Reformation, civil authorities are ordained of God to restrain evil (Rom.13:1–7). Subjects are commanded to obey the state except in those cases when such obedience would entail disobedience to God. If there is a conflict between the demands of Caesar and those of God (as, for example, in empower-worship), one ought always to "obey God rather than men" (Act.5:29). In such instances, however, resistance to the state is limited to civil disobedience.

In the sixteenth century Calvin added one important qualification to the traditional teaching of obedience to civil authorities when he affirmed the duty of lower magistrates to resist the violence and cruelty of tyrants. This duty resides in their office as magistrates who are also divinely appointed to protect the liberty of the people.[19] At the same time, Calvin insisted that such a duty extends only to magistrates and not to private individuals; subjects are commanded only to obey except in those cases when passive disobedience is required for the sake of conscience.

Based upon a covenantal understanding of society, seventeenth-century Puritans in England (Baxter) and New England (Winthrop, Davenport, Cotton, Hooker) held that all government rests upon consent of the people. According to Baxter, the contract between subjects and rulers is founded upon a more fundamental covenant between the people and God, namely, that they would be ruled in accordance with the law of God.[20] Appealing to this underlying covenant, the people reserved certain rights and liberties to themselves when they established civil governments. Appeal to such rights and liberties served primarily to protect the people against tyrannical and arbitrary government. It was on this basis that Puritans such as Cromwell and Baxter justified participation in the revolt against Charles I. Similar appeals also provided the basis for political revolution in Scotland in the sixteenth century (John Knox) and in pre-Revolutionary America.

NATURAL RIGHTS

Although Puritanism in England was deeply rooted in the Reformed tradition, it also drew both upon medieval notions of natural law and upon contemporary conceptions of natural rights. The first systematic statement of a doctrine of natural rights was set forth by the Dutch Protestant theologian and jurist, Hugo Grotius, early in the sixteenth century.[21] According to Grotius, certain moral requirements can be known on the basis of reason without belief in God and special revelation. These norms and values are grounded in human nature; as such they are included in the law of nature. Human beings are born free and equal; they are also social by nature and desire to live together in peaceful and cooperative forms of society. Reason also teaches that in order to achieve that end, laws and institutions which protect the natural equality and freedom of all are needed. Through birth all individuals have a natural right to exercise control over their own property and resist the use of arbitrary force.

Following Grotius, Thomas Hobbes and John Locke developed the idea of natural rights in two radically different ways, based upon different conceptions of human nature. For Hobbes, the natural state of humanity is a condition of war of "everyone against everyone," arising out of the clash of competing forms of self-interest.[22] In the state of nature – prior to all agreements, laws, and customs – each individual is endowed with a right "to all things," including the bodies and possessions of others. Hobbes grounds this right in the first and fundamental law of nature, which requires both the seeking of peace and self-preservation. Since these ends cannot be attained in the state of nature, reason also teaches – the second law of nature – that individuals ought to surrender their natural right to all things to an absolutist state. With the establishment of such a state, individuals no longer possess any rights against the tyranny of the state.

Based upon different conceptions of human nature and the law of nature from Hobbes, Locke developed a doctrine of natural rights which are not only inherent but also inalienable. As such they provides a continuing basis for resistance against all forms of tyranny and political oppression. For Locke, not only are all persons created free and equal; they are also social by nature. Instead of a condition of perpetual warfare, the natural state of humanity was "a state of peace, good will, mutual assistance, and preservation."[23] Despite its idyllic character, it was also a state of insecurity and anxiety. Thus men were driven by convenience, necessity, and inclination to establish political societies and institute governments. When these were formed, individuals still retained the basic liberty and equality with which they were endowed at birth.

For Locke, natural rights are based not upon self-interest but upon certain obligations grounded in the law of nature, which contains two fundamental precepts, namely, the duty to preserve oneself and the duty to preserve others. Since the duty of self-preservation is universal, all people have a corresponding right to those conditions which are necessary for its fulfillment. The most basic of these conditions are life, liberty, and property (possessions). Locke calls these "natural rights." Not only do they constitute protections against wilful and arbitrary harm to any member of society; they also establish an obligation to provide a subsistence level of food and shelter to those in dire need. Since the earth is given to humanity in common, all have a natural right (which is prior to conventional rights) to property sufficient for their self-preservation. Hence, for Locke, charity is – like justice – both a right and a duty: it is a right on the part of the needy and a duty on the part of those who have "enough and to spare."

Although human beings are inclined by nature to form societies, they exist first of all as individuals and only secondarily as members of society. Based on this underlying view of human nature, Locke's conception of natural rights is essentially rationalistic and individualistic. Rights pertain primarily to the liberties which individuals need in order to fulfill their duty to preserve themselves and humankind. Locke acknowledges the need for other, more communal forms of virtue, but he is unable either to demonstrate the rationality of the latter or to develop their richer meaning on the basis of reason alone. On account of the tensions and ambiguities in his thought, Locke's notions of natural law and natural rights were construed in America in the seventeenth and eighteenth centuries largely in individualistic terms. As a result, the more communal dimensions of his vision of justice were displaced by the more rationalistic and individualistic heritage of natural rights.[24] This was true of his impact upon both religious and secular thought.

As noted in chapter four, the crisis in federal theology in the seventeenth and eighteenth centuries reflected an underlying moral crisis in society as a whole. The American Republic was grounded upon a covenant among the people themselves. The Constitution represented a promise of justice. As promise, it embodied a commitment to justice and "the general welfare." At the same time it also included a Bill of Rights. Thus, within the promise of justice the tension between individual rights and the public good remains. The purpose of the Constitution is stated in terms of the well-being of the people as a whole; yet the document itself seems primarily concerned with the protection of political and civil liberties of individuals rather than the provision of assistance in the attainment of the general good.

HUMAN RIGHTS

The natural rights tradition was a major source of the modern human rights movement, which has also been shaped by other philosophical and religious influences, including not only those of the West and the East, but also those of the Third World. These traditions differ widely in their interpretations of the ground of human worth, but they have been united in affirming the fundamental dignity of all persons as the basis for human rights. While the United Nations was able to agree upon a "Universal Declaration of Human Rights" (1948), the Declaration itself does not offer any justification for such rights. Instead, the Preamble to that document begins with recognition of the "inherent dignity" of all persons along with certain "equal and inalienable rights" which are possessed by "all members of the human family."[25]

From a theological perspective, two features of the Declaration and the subsequent international covenants on human rights (1966) are particularly striking. One is impressed, first of all, with the extent to which our contemporary understanding of human rights has been immeasurably enriched by the pluralistic context in which the movement developed. This is particularly true in regard to the increased recognition of the relativity of rights claims when considered in a global context. Viewed in that context, there has been a growing perception both of the diversity and also of the interdependence of human rights, including political, civil, economic, social and cultural rights. At the same time, however, the claims of an inherent human dignity and the inalienability of such rights are in effect left suspended in mid-air, because of the failure to provide religious and philosophical justification for them. As a result, the rights which do emerge are cut off from their origin in the essentially religious beliefs and traditions from which they sprang and which are needed for their continued nurture and support.[26]

In a pluralistic society, it is necessary to base rights-claims upon a general consensus of commonly held beliefs and values. Such claims are in reality the product of the interaction of a number of distinct moral traditions. Moreover, particular rights – for example, religious liberty and freedom of speech – are often interpreted differently in various traditions and diverse cultural settings. Hence, public space is needed for ongoing debate concerning the nature, the basis, and the concrete meaning of human rights, including the relationship between individual rights and the common good.[27]

COVENANT: HUMAN RIGHTS AND THE COMMON GOOD

What, then, can a covenantal understanding of justice contribute to the contemporary discussion of human rights? First of all, standing as it does in the Reformed tradition, the notion of covenant places the debate in the theocentric context of God's universal covenant with humanity. Viewed from a biblical perspective, rights claims are based upon the twin concepts of the "image of God" and covenant. Indeed, the full meaning of the *imago Dei* comes to expression only in the covenant as a symbol of the divine purpose in the creation of humanity, namely, that all persons should live together in covenant relationships both with God and with one another.[28] Taken by itself this metaphor has often been interpreted in quite individualistic terms. On the basis of their shared "image of God," all persons are said to be created free and equal. In the natural rights tradition these qualities are interpreted in terms of the capacity for reason and the duty to obey the moral law (the law of nature). In the biblical doctrine of creation, covenant not only presupposes liberty and equality, but also points to their fulfillment in community.

Individuals come into being as members of community. They are bound together by ties of mutual dependence, kinship, affection, and sympathy. To say that these relationships are covenantal is to say that they rest upon trust or the promise of mutual fidelity. Such promises may be either explicit, as in marriage, oaths of public office, and membership in churches, or implicit, as in relationships between parents and children, physicians and patients, and citizenship by birth. Covenant makes use of contracts and rights, but beyond these it points to the under-lying relationships of dependence, obligation and need in which contracts and rights are embedded. Covenant finally demands faithfulness to one's neighbor.

Covenant provides the basis for a distinction between universal human rights grounded in God's covenant with humanity, and special rights grounded in particular covenants. Universal rights refer to the most fundamental conditions which are necessary for the fulfillment of human life. Such rights are inclusive: they are bestowed upon all persons by birth. They are also inalienable; they can neither be given nor taken away. Human rights may be either negative or positive. Negative rights refer to protections against unjustified interference (immunities); they include, for example, the right to life, liberty, personal security, freedom of speech and assembly, and freedom of worship. Positive rights refer to rights of assistance in the provision of goods and services such as food, shelter, gainful employment, a basic level of medical care, and education.

As just noted, special rights differ from universal human rights in that they are grounded in particular covenants such as marriage, parenthood, citizenship, membership in churches, and physician–patient relationships. Compared with universal rights, special rights are relatively exclusive; they pertain to membership in particular groups. Like universal rights, special rights may be either negative or positive. It is useful to distinguish between inclusive and special rights, but special rights are based upon (and presuppose) the former.

Rights are indispensable criteria of justice; however, rights are not absolute. They are limited, for example, by scarce resources, by the prevailing state of technology, and by emergency condi-tions such as natural calamities and war. Rights frequently conflict with other rights, including both those of individuals and those of groups. Rights must continually be interpreted and defended in light of changing historical and cultural circumstances. Rights must also be applied to particular cases, and conflicts must be resolved through an ordering of rights or through appeals to equity and the common good.

Viewed in terms of covenant, human rights are set within a

framework of obligation and duty. As Miller noted, the great end of covenant theology was to develop a concept of mutual responsibility in which law and the good were united, in which attainment of the good was made conditional upon obedience to the fundamental moral law, which was discernible by reason but more fully disclosed through revelation. In their attempt to achieve this goal, Puritans such as Ames and Perkins drew upon classical and Thomistic conceptions of natural law and a common good. There was a great deal of similarity between the Puritan and Thomistic conceptions of the general good, although in covenantal thought this was attained through obedience to law, whereas in the classical tradition it was attained primarily through the practice of virtue. Typically, in Puritanism the well-being of the whole was called the "public good" (Baxter, Willard); in the natural law tradition it was called the "common good."[29]

In its historical origin the "common good" was a more richly communal concept than the "public good." In the end, however, both images proved to be unstable syntheses of the public and private good. In Puritanism, as we have seen, natural law came to be interpreted largely in the more rationalistic and abstract terms of the law of nature, and the public good came to be defined in individualistic and utilitarian terms as a collection of private goods. Similarly, in modern Roman Catholicism prior to Vatican II, Catholic social teachings were justified primarily by appeals to the law of nature.[30] Beginning with the encyclical of Pope Leo XIII, *Rerum Novarum* (1891), emphasis in the official documents of the church began to shift away from the ideal of Christendom to the transcendent dignity of the human person, grounded in the *imago Dei*.[31] Emphasis upon personal dignity led to an individualistic interpretation of human rights. As a result, civil and political rights, particularly religious liberty, were understood in negative terms of noninterference. Economic and social rights referred to particular social circumstances which were prerequisite primarily for personal dignity.

Since Vatican II, more direct appeal to the central symbols of the church (for example, the Eucharist) and use of biblical teachings – including the love commandment, the action and

teachings of Jesus, and the motifs of covenant and liberation –
have "stimulated a new dynamism and critical spirit" in
Catholic social teachings.[32] Beginning with the decade of the
1980s, human rights have been based increasingly upon the
retrieval of a more communal interpretation of the "common
good." Thus understood, rights are the "minimum conditions
for life in community."[33] Both human dignity and human rights
are now viewed as essentially social; they are also mutually
interdependent. Neither can be adequately understood in isolation from the other.

In contrast to the natural rights tradition, both covenant and
the common good are based upon communal conceptions of
human nature and human fulfillment. In covenantal terms, the
moral bonds of community are essentially promissory and
obligatory; in Catholic social teaching, they are essentially
teleological, based upon the natural inclination of each to seek
his or her personal fulfillment in and through that of the
community as a whole. As root metaphors of community both
covenant and the common good are needed to interpret each
other and also to nurture the full meaning of justice from a
theological perspective. Both contain resources for a far deeper
and richer vision of the human good than liberty alone provides.
In both, rights are set within the more inclusive context of
justice which includes not only rights but also obligations, not
only law but also virtue. In both traditions rights include
participation in political and economic forms of power, shared
responsibility, and mutual accountability for social outcomes.
Both covenant and the common good point beyond rights to the
basis of the latter in community and to the fulfillment of justice
in love.

CRITERIA OF DISTRIBUTIVE JUSTICE

In addition to rights, justice also includes fairness in the exchange
and distribution of many different kinds of goods. While distributive justice may be defined at the most abstract level in terms of
one basic universal principle such as equality (desert, need, social
utility, ability, legal entitlement), other moral criteria are also

needed in the application of this norm to different kinds of goods in particular situations. Thus, Walzer, for example, uses the term "complex equality" to describe the different meanings of equality in different sets of relationships.[34] Similarly, he uses the concept "spheres of justice" to distinguish between various kinds of goods, the distinctive sets of relationships in and through which these goods are exchanged or distributed, and the particular moral criteria which are appropriate to the various forms (spheres) of distributive justice.

The free market, for instance, provides a just or fair basis for the exchange of certain kinds of elective, or optional, goods and services. But even here, additional criteria such as relative equality, truthfulness in disclosure, and liberty of both parties to the exchange are also important criteria of justice. Other goods – awards and honors – are justly bestowed on the basis of merit. Though merit is the essential criterion of such honors and awards, other standards are also needed to assure fair procedures in the award process itself, including the establishment of such awards, provision of opportunities to attain them, and the selection process itself. In contrast to those goods which may be distributed fairly on the basis of reciprocity or merit, certain other goods are essential for human life in community. Among these are a safe natural environment, a basic level of medical care, education, and access to gainful employment. Such goods are fundamental goods; they are also public goods. Not only are they essential for the well-being of each individual; they are also necessary for the well-being of the community as a whole. Understood in covenantal terms, such goods ought to be distributed primarily on the basis of need. Since *need* is a highly subjective and relative standard, however, more specific criteria are necessary both for the identification and for the ordering of competing needs.

Medical care provides a paradigmatic example of a communal good which ought to be distributed by the community equally among its members on the basis of need. This obligation is implicit not only in the covenantal basis of community itself but also in the practice of medicine as a profession.[35] From its beginning, as Melvin Konner notes, health care has always been

– and continues to be – a "public good, and its guardianship a public trust."[36]

In the United States today the covenantal tradition in the practice of medicine exists in uneasy tension with the dominant free market model based upon contractual stipulations and fee-for-service calculations. Due to the rapid growth of medical research and technology in the period since World War II together with the increasing institutionalization and bureaucracy of the health care system, there has been growing recognition of the communal dimensions of modern medicine.[37] Not only is medical research publicly funded to a large extent; health care itself is provided through a network of institutions which are supported by the community as a whole. As a result, the horizons of modern medicine have expanded far beyond the dyadic relationship between physician and patient; the practice of medicine now includes teams of health care providers and a growing perception of health as human wholeness. These transformations both of the practice of medicine and of the parameters of health care have been accompanied by rapidly escalating costs, profound demographic changes (particularly the aging of the population with expanding need for long-term critical care), the impact of AIDS, and the widespread use of addictive drugs.

The mounting crisis in health care in the United States has focused attention on three major issues of distributive justice: (1) accessibility, (2) the level of universal coverage, and (3) the allocation of scarce resources. These issues are interrelated. At present an estimated 34–37 million Americans do not have medical insurance. Approximately 13–14 per cent of the Gross National Product is currently being spent on health care; and this percentage has been rising steadily in recent years. Since national resources are limited, greater attention needs to be given to their allocation among such areas as nutrition and preventative medicine, mental illness, holistic health, and critical and long-term care. In addition, many medical goods – transplant organs, sophisticated technology, and certain drugs, for example – will continue to be scarce.

In relation to accessibility, the fundamental question is whether everyone should have access to a basic level of medical care

without regard to one's ability to pay. In 1983 a Presidential
Commission concluded that society has a moral obligation to
assure that all citizens have "equitable access" to "an adequate
level of care without excessive burdens."[38] The Commission
described this level as a "floor below which no one ought to fall."
From a covenantal perspective the moral right to a basic level of
care is grounded in the equality of human worth and in the
recognition that health care is not only a fundamental good but
also a public good. Such a right, however, is neither absolute nor
unconditional. Health care is both a mutual responsibility and a
mutually shared good.

The question of the level of care is implicit in the question of
access. The ideas of "equitable access," "an adequate level of
care," and a "floor" suggest that the criteria of equalilty and need
are relational rather than fixed norms. Equality itself is limited by
need. Equality does not mean, for example, that everyone should
receive a heart transplant whether or not everyone needs one.
Need is also limited in a similar way by scarcity of resources.
Factors which contribute to such scarcity include the escalating
costs of health care generally, the development of new therapies
and new forms of medical technology, and competition with
other goods. At the local institutional level, claims to scarce
resources based upon equality and need must of necessity be
limited and ordered by appeals to other criteria such as equity,
proportionality, and the common good.

Consideration of scarcity brings us face to face not only with
the limits of equality and need in relation to individual patients; it
also raises the question of the allocation of scarce resources
among various types of treatment. Health means the well-being
and appropriate functioning of the person as a whole in the
context of finitude, suffering, and death.[39] It includes physical or
biological well-being; it also includes psychological, social, and
spiritual well-being. Medical care should be balanced with other
health needs. Moreover, as noted above, within the context of
medical care itself greater priority should be given to prevention
rather than curative medicine. Such a re-ordering of priorities is
prerequisite for any effective control over escalating costs; it
would also be more efficacious in terms of outcomes. Similarly,

from a covenantal perspective, greater attention should be given to human finitude, quality of life, and proportionality in decisions concerning termination of treatment of terminally ill patients.

JUSTICE AS VOCATION

In the context of covenant the work of justice is most adequately understood in terms of vocation. As God's chosen people Israel was summoned to do justice patterned after the divine righteousness. In the Reformed tradition civil magistracy is, in the words of Calvin, "a calling not only holy and legitimate, but far the most sacred and honourable in human life."[40] While Calvin was speaking of civil magistrates generally, he preferred either an aristocratic government or a mixture of aristocracy and democracy to monarchy. Government by the many was needed, he believed, to provide protection against the vices and imperfections of kings. Through "their mutual assistance and admonition" the many are able to achieve a fuller insight into the proper ends of government and greater protection against injustice than monarchs.

Both in England and in America the idea of civil magistracy as a vocation was expressed by the Puritans in their covenantal conception of civil societies.[41] The citizens who covenanted together to form a political body had an obligation to participate in the governance of the commonwealth. As a matter of conscience, it was their duty to hold magistrates accountable for the public good and to guard against injustice. Justice was the great end of government, and justice meant the common good.[42]

As a vocation justice includes both character and law ("the rules of justice"). On the one hand, it requires integrity, trustworthiness, prudence, and commitment to the public good on the part of rulers. On the other hand, just laws are also necessary to provide more impartial criteria of justice in view of human finitude and particularly in view of human sin. As Aristotle perceived, the just person may do unjust acts. Hence, it is not sufficient to say that justice is what the just person does. From a covenantal perspective, moreover, justice cannot be finally defined in terms of the values and norms of any historical group.

In its highest and most inclusive form, justice points to a transcendent norm in terms of which all systems of human justice are ultimately measured. In biblical terms, justice is a requirement of God's righteousness not only within Israel but also among all nations. The fundamental structure of human life is the same for all peoples, and all participate in the same ultimate moral order. Hence, there is some knowledge of justice based in Creation, although such knowledge has been perverted by self-centeredness, pride, and idolatry.

While justice has traditionally been associated with God's restraining or ordering activity in Protestant ethics, it is also related to his creative will and to the structures of human fulfillment in community. The promise of such fulfillment is present in the biblical ideas of covenant and the Kingdom of God. It is also present in the notion of a divine commonwealth in Reformed theology and in the ideas of natural law and a common good in Catholic thought. In a democratic form of government justice requires the participation of all the citizens in the determination of the public good, and also in its distribution.[43]

THE RENEWAL AND TRANSFORMATION OF JUSTICE

In a democratic society justice is based upon the promise of liberty and equality. The ways in which these are understood and applied differ with changing historical and cultural circumstances. In a democracy the citizens are free to govern themselves. At its most fundamental level, equality means that each citizen has a right to vote and that this right is distributed equally: one-citizen-one-vote. Democracy is the political way in which power is entrusted by the people to elected representatives to be used for the public good. As Walzer has observed, in a democracy equality means an equal right to vote and participate in the opportunities and occasions of power, not equality of power itself.[44] Equality presupposes freedom from domination by hereditary and arbitrary forms of power. It means the right to continue to participate in the struggle for justice irrespective of the outcomes of particular elections. Such equality includes the ballot; it also includes the rights of free speech, assembly, and petition.

In the political sphere the vote is a fundamental expression of equality because it symbolizes membership, and it gives concrete meaning to democratic participation in governance. For most Americans at the close of the eighteenth century, however, liberty and equality remained unfulfilled promises. The franchise was limited largely to adult white males who met certain tax-paying or property qualifications. Women were excluded, as were Native Americans and slaves. Even after the franchise was extended to these groups, the struggle for full membership and equality of participation has continued to the present day. Meantime, despite its aristocratic overtones, many members of these groups have seen in the Constitution promise of their own equality and full membership in the political community. This vision has provided the basis for women's suffrage and the civil rights movement in the present century, including the rights of Native Americans. Fuller achievement of liberty and equality depends also upon more profound understandings of these norms, upon the empowerment of marginalized groups, and upon the emergence of new opportunities and occasions for their realization.

Similar polarities and tensions have also been present in our national life in its underlying conceptions of natural rights and the public good. These conflicting ideas are rooted fundamentally in competing notions of the relationship between individuals and society. The biblical and Puritan covenantal tradition has provided a basically communal paradigm of human nature and civil society. As we have seen, this image was also reinforced in important ways by "civic humanism" and republican virtue. At the same time, however, it has existed in tension and conflict with other more atomistic and voluntaristic images of society based upon contract and interest.

Not only have the polarities and tensions between these paradigms been present in American democracy from its beginnings; they were also present in Locke's idea of a social compact. Ontologically, the social compact was rooted in human interdependence; morally, it was based upon the law of nature and the duty of self-preservation. While Locke saw the ultimate goal of

the government as the protection of "the peace, safety, and public
good of the people," he interpreted this goal in essentially
individualistic terms. For him, justice meant the protection of the
rights of individuals to pursue their own well-being and happiness
without interference. Along with the duty of justice, it will be
recalled, Locke also recognized a duty of charity on the part of
those who have "enough and to spare"; such charity was limited,
however, to the provision of subsistence for the needy.

For Locke, justice includes the duty to preserve others as well
as oneself; at the same time, however, a strong commitment to
the general good, which is present in the classical tradition of
justice and in the covenantal conception of the public good, is
lacking. There is also a similar ambiguity and tension regarding
the meaning of trust both in Locke and in common political
usage. Both in Locke and in covenantal thought trust is the basic
bond of society; yet the term itself has different meanings in the
two contexts. In both instances trust signifies trustworthiness and
fidelity to the promise which is implicit in a compact or covenant;
a basic difference arises, however, out of different understandings
of the public good as the end of government. For Locke, trust
means faithfulness in the protection of the lives, liberties, and
possessions of individuals; in covenantal thought, it means faithfulness to the promise to promote the good of the whole even at
the expense of private interest.

Just as the covenant conception of community informed and
shaped the life of Israel at its most fundamental level, so it also
constituted the basic structure of Puritan society in England and
America in the seventeenth and eighteenth centuries. In the
course of the eighteenth century, the idea became increasingly
secularized; as such it provided the most important paradigm for
the self-understanding of the new nation as a people. Secularization of the political community did not mean that the religious
roots of the idea and faith in an overruling Divine Providence
were unimportant or expendable. It meant, rather, that church
and state would be separate and that there would be no
established religion or church. Within the context of an officially
secular state, the free exercise of religion was protected. Within
this context the biblical/Reformed (Puritan) symbol of covenant

entered into our national heritage. As such it provided – and continues to provide – an indispensable metaphor for our self-understanding as a people under the sovereignty and providence of God.

Understood in terms of promise, covenant provides a basis for the positive, creative work of justice in the building of community and in the creation of new forms of community. It provides the foundation also for greater realizations of liberty and equality based upon the common dignity which all share through creation in the "image of God." In the light of that fundamental equality, covenant also seeks the inclusion of all as full members of society. Since liberty and equality are relational rather than absolute, the struggle to achieve them always remains incomplete in human history.[45] Moreover, as Walzer suggests, the idea of equality is itself a complex notion. "Mutual respect and a shared self-respect" are both the deep strengths of complex equality and also the source of its possible endurance.[46] Such respect is deeply rooted in a theological conception of human dignity grounded in creation. Equality is also expressed in the form of human rights.

In its understanding of the depth and pervasiveness of sin, covenant also provides a basis for the restraining and ordering task of justice in a democratic society. In the words of Reinhold Niebuhr, "Man's capacity for justice makes democracy possible; but man's inclination to injustice makes democracy necessary."[47] Virtue alone – whether of the masses or of an aristocratic elite – was insufficient, the Founders believed, to assure the well-being and survival of the Republic. Hence they provided for a separation of legislative, judicial, and executive powers together with a system of checks and balances within the Constitution itself. In the end, there is ultimate accountability of the elected representatives to the people – all within the framework of laws which are binding upon ruler and ruled alike.

Institutional structures based upon law do not make virtue unnecessary either on the part of the subjects or on the part of the rulers. In the republican tradition hope for the inculcation and renewal of virtue rested upon moral education and faith in the regenerative effects of republican government itself upon the character of the people.[48] The Calvinist clergy, on the other hand, saw in the Revolutionary crisis a call to repentance and hope for renewal based upon grace. While both groups recognized the necessity for virtue, they differed radically in their understandings of both the sources of evil and the basis for hope for renewal and regeneration. In the conflict between these views, the religious perception of evil and the corresponding need for institutional restraints upon injustice proved more realistic than the rationalistic and humanistic insights. In the context of separation of church and state, voluntary religious groups continue to contribute in profound ways both to the formation of the character of the people and to the shaping of institutional forms of justice.

Finally, in its covenantal form justice provides a basis for the transformation of law and justice itself by self-giving love. Aristotle noted that judicial justice involves more than the strict application of just rules: If justice in the full sense of the term is to be done, there is need for equity in the administration of the law. Moreover, friendship rather than justice constitutes the fundamental bond of the *polis*. In Christian ethics there is an even closer relationship between justice and love. Here the aim of justice is not only the preservation of existing forms of community, but also the restoration of broken community through the discovery of new possibilities which are hidden from justice alone. Amid the brokenness and conflicts of human history, the highest form of justice is reconciling justice.[49] Such justice transforms not only the justice of individual agents but also the justice of communities – not only the quality of justice which the citizens embody as persons but also the laws and practices of the community. Love makes use of secular forms of reciprocal, distributive, and juridical justice in the earthly city, but love transforms them by directing them beyond justice proper to the restoration of broken relationships and to the creation of new and fuller forms of community. Such love is necessary in order to prevent the highest forms of human justice from turning into new forms of injustice; at the deepest level, it is essential for the overcoming of the universal human tendencies toward self-centeredness and idolatry, which are the roots of injustice.

Notes

1 INTRODUCTION

1 Harold J. Berman, *Law and Revolution: The Formation of the Western Legal Tradition* (Cambridge, Mass.: Harvard University Press, 1983), pp. 529–530.

2 *Ibid.*, pp. 534–536.

3 Harold J. Berman, "Religious Foundations of Law in the West: An Historical Perspective," *Journal of Law and Religion* 1:1 (1983), p. 5.

4 *Ibid.*, p. 43.

5 Berman, *Law and Revolution*, p. vii. On the interaction of law and religion, see also the following collection of essays by Berman: *Faith and Order: The Reconciliation of Law and Religion* (Atlanta, Georgia: Scholars Press, 1993).

6 Berman, *Law and Revolution*, pp. 40–41.

7 *Ibid.*, p. 41.

8 *Ibid.*, p. 11.

9 *Ibid.*, p. 534.

10 See for example, Emil Brunner, *Justice and the Social Order* (London: Lutterworth Press, 1945).

11 On the revision of traditional natural law theory in recent Roman Catholic thought, see the following: Josef Fuchs, S. J., *Natural Law: A Theological Investigation* (New York: Sheed and Ward, 1965); Charles E. Curran, "Natural Law and Contemporary Moral Theology," in Curran, *Contemporary Problems in Moral Theology* (Notre Dame, Indiana: Fides Publishers, Inc., 1970), pp. 97–158; Josef Gremillion (ed.), *The Gospel of Peace and Justice: Catholic Social Teaching Since Pope John* (Maryknoll, New York: Orbis Books, 1976), esp. pp. 7–10 and 531–567; and Charles E. Curran and Richard A. McCormick, S. J. (eds.), *Natural Law and Theology* (*Readings in Moral Theology*, No. 7) (New York: Paulist Press, 1991).

12 Alasdair MacIntyre, *After Virtue: A Study in Moral Theology* (Notre Dame, Indiana: University of Notre Dame Press, 1981), pp. 227–237.

13 Milner S. Ball, *The Promise of American Law: A Theological, Humanistic View of Legal Process* (Athens, Georgia: The University of Georgia Press, 1981); Michael Walzer, *Exodus and Revolution* (New York: Basic Books, Inc., 1985); and Donald S. Lutz, *The Origins of American Constitutionalism* (Baton Rouge, Louisiana: Louisiana State University Press, 1988).

14 See Robert N. Bellah, Richard Madsen, William M. Sullivan, Ann Swidler, and Steven M. Tipton, *Habits of the Heart: Individualism and Commitment in American Life* (Berkeley: University of California Press, 1985), pp. 154ff., 292.

2 THE CLASSICAL TRADITION OF VIRTUE

1 Alasdair MacIntyre, *After Virtue: A Study in Moral Theology* (Notre Dame, Indiana: University of Notre Dame Press, 1981), p. 227.
2 *Ibid.*, p. 143.
3 *Ibid.*, p. 236.
4 *Ibid.*, pp. 244–245.
5 *Ibid.*, p. 245.
6 *Ibid.*, p. 237.
7 *Ibid.*
8 *Ibid.*, pp. 194–205.
9 Alasdair MacIntyre, *Whose Justice? Which Rationality?* (Notre Dame, Indiana: University of Notre Dame Press, 1988). See esp. pp. 349–403.
10 *Ibid.*, pp. 326–327.
11 *Ibid.*, p. 396.
12 If MacIntyre's proposal concerning the construction of local forms of community had been stated in theological terms, it would have represented a form of "Christ Against Culture" morality described by H. Richard Niebuhr in *Christ and Culture* (New York: Harper & Brothers, 1951), pp. 45–82. Hauerwas' ethic also resembles this type of theological ethics; Gustafson, however, is more closely akin to the Thomistic synthesis of morality based on faith and reason as well as the synthesis of virtue and law.
13 Stanley Hauerwas, *A Community of Character* (Notre Dame, Indiana: University of Notre Dame Press, 1981), p. 128; compare Stanley Hauerwas, *Vision and Virtue* (Notre Dame, Indiana: Fides Publishers, Inc., 1974), pp. 228–240.
14 Hauerwas, *A Community of Character*, pp. 36–52. See, also, Stanley Hauerwas, *After Christendom? How the Church is to Behave if Freedom, Justice, and a Christian Nation Are Bad Ideas* (Nashville: Abingdon Press, 1991), pp. 148–152.

15 Hauerwas, *Community of Character*, p. 109. See, also, Stanley Hauerwas, *The Peaceable Kingdom* (Notre Dame, Indiana: University of Notre Dame Press, 1983), pp. 99–102; *After Christendom?*, pp. 21–22, 44. Compare Stanley Hauerwas and William H. Willimon, *Resident Aliens: Life in the Christian Colony* (Nashville: Abingdon Press, 1989), pp. 43–47; 82–83.

16 Hauerwas not only rejects the characterization of his ecclesiology as a form of sectarianism ("Christ Against Culture"); more fundamentally, he rejects the underlying presuppositions upon which Niebuhr's study, *Christ and Culture*, is based. Hauerwas describes the latter as "a prime example of repressive tolerance," based upon Niebuhr's own liberal theology and his commitment to theological pluralism (Hauerwas, *Resident Aliens*, p. 41). Hauerwas fails to give adequate attention both to the dialectical relationship of the various types to each other in Niebuhr's analysis and also to Niebuhr's insistence upon the eschatological character of the transformationist hope, based upon God's redemptive action in human history.

In contrast to Niebuhr's typology of theological ethics, Hauerwas identifies his own ecclesiology much more closely with John Howard Yoder's concept of the "confessing church" (*Resident Aliens*, pp. 44–45). His emphasis is upon the "peculiarity", or distinctiveness, of Christian ethics and upon the church as a "countercultural phenomenon" (*ibid.*, pp. 71; 30).

17 Hauerwas, *Community of Character*, p. 109; *After Christendom?*, pp. 93–111. See, also, *Resident Aliens*, pp. 30; 69–92.

18. See Hauerwas, *The Peaceable Kingdom*, pp. 106–111; compare *Vision and Virtue*, p. 240, n. 41.

19 Hauerwas, *Community of Character*, p. 254; *Peaceable Kingdom*, pp. 102–106.

20 Hauerwas, *Vision and Virtue*, p. 219.

21 Hauerwas, *Peaceable Kingdom*, pp. 104; 114.

22 Hauerwas, *Vision and Virtue*, pp. 231–240.

23 Hauerwas, *Community of Character*, p. 3; compare *Resident Aliens*, pp. 49–68; 144–171.

24 Hauerwas, *Community of Character*, p. 128; *Peaceable Kingdom*, pp. 99–106; *After Christendom?* ("The Politics of Justice: Why Justice is a Bad Idea for Christians"), pp. 45–68.

25 Hauerwas, *Community of Character*, p. 100. See also, *Peaceable Kingdom*, pp. 24–34.

26 Stanley Hauerwas, *Character and the Christian Life* (San Antonio, Texas: Trinity University Press, 1975), pp. 14–16.

27 James M. Gustafson, *Ethics from a Theocentric Perspective*, 2 vols. (The

University of Chicago Press, 1981–1984), vol. II, *Ethics and Theology*, pp. 1–2; compare pp. 146; 279. For a concise "profile" of theocentric ethics, see *ibid.*, pp. 1–22. Compare James M. Gustafson, *Can Ethics Be Christian?* (The University of Chicago Press, 1975), pp. 156–157.

28 James M. Gustafson, *Protestant and Roman Catholic Ethics: Prospects for Rapprochement* (The University of Chicago Press, 1978), pp. 95–137.

29 Gustafson, *Can Ethics Be Christian?*; see, esp., chapter 2: "The 'Sort of Person' One Is," pp. 25–47.

30 Gustafson, *Ethics from a Theocentric Perspective*, II, pp. 292–319. Compare *Can Ethics Be Christian?*, pp. 1–24; 158.

31 Gustafson, *Ethics from a Theocentric Perspective*, II, pp. 315–319. See also, *Can Ethics Be Christian?* pp. 145–168.

32 Gustafson, *Ethics from a Theocentric Perspective*, II, pp. 315–319.

33 James M. Gustafson, *Christian Ethics and the Community* (Philadelphia: Pilgrim Press, 1971), pp. 153–163; 202. See also, *Ethics from a Theocentric Perspective*, I, pp. 339–340.

For an incisive analysis of the moral bases of marriage and family in the underlying interpersonal, organic, and social relationships upon which these institutions rest, see *Ethics from a Theocentric Perspective*, II, pp. 153–184. While the moral ties which are present in marriage and the family are interpreted fundamentally in terms of virtue, these (moral) ties also include covenantal bonds, duties, and obligations.

34 Gustafson, *Christian Ethics and the Community*, pp. 172–175; 199–202.

35 MacIntyre, *After Virtue*, p. 226.

36 Aristotle, *The Nicomachean Ethics*, trans. J. E. C. Weldon (Buffalo, New York: Prometheus Books, 1987), p. 146 (Bk. V, ch. 3).

37 Georgio Del Vecchio, *Justice: An Historical and Philosophical Essay* (Edinburgh University Press, 1952), p. 54. Del Vecchio further notes that this characteristic of justice has been "reasserted by all subsequent writers who have thought deeply on the subject."

38 Aristotle, *Nicomachean Ethics*, p. 146 (Bk. V, ch. 3).

39 *Ibid.*, p. 151 (Bk. V, ch. 6).

40 Anton C. Pegis (ed.), *The Basic Writings of Saint Thomas Aquinas*, 2 vols. (New York: Random House, 1945), II, p. 830.

41 Thomas Aquinas, *Summa Theologiae*, vol. XXXVII, *Justice* (2a2ae. 57–62). Latin text, English translation, Introduction, Notes and Glossary, edited by Thomas Gilby (Cambridge: Blackfriars, 1975), p. 31.

42 *Ibid.*, p. 33.

43 *Ibid.*, p. 51.

44 Pegis, *Basic Writings of Aquinas*, II. pp. 460–461.

45 Josef Pieper, *The Four Cardinal Virtues* (Notre Dame, Indiana: University of Notre Dame Press, 1966), pp. 70–75.
46 *Ibid.*, pp. 54–63.
47 *Ibid.*, p. 99.
48 *Ibid.*, p. 89
49 Francis H. Eterovich (ed.), *Aristotle's Nicomachean Ethics: Commentary and Analysis* (Washington, D.C.: University Press of America, 1980), pp. 90–91.
50 Pieper, *Four Cardinal Virtues*, p. 46.
51 Aristotle, *Nicomachean Ethics* (1987), p. 142 (Bk. v, ch. 1).
52 *Ibid.*, pp. 164–165; 171–172 (Bk. v, ch. 10).
53 *Ibid.*, p. 167 (Bk. v, ch. 10).
54 *Ibid.*, p. 168 (Bk. v, ch. 10).
55 Aristotle, *Politics* (New York: Random House, The Modern Library edn., 1943), pp. 149.
56 *Ibid.*, pp. 320–337.
57 Aquinas, *Summa Theologiae*, XXXVII, p. 21.
58 *Ibid.*, p. 27.
59 *Ibid.*, p. 49.
60 See C. Perelman, *The Idea of Justice and the Problem of Argument* (London: Routledge & Paul, 1963), pp. 61–78.
61 As Pieper observes, the recognition of the primacy of the *right* led Aquinas to place his discussion of the latter before his treatise on justice in the *Summa Theologica*. Pieper, *Four Cardinal Virtues*, p. 46.
62 Aristotle, *Nicomachean Ethics* (1987), pp. 178–181 (Bk. v, ch. 14).
63 *Ibid.*, p. 254 (Bk. VIII, ch. 1).
64 *Ibid.*, pp. 260–269 (Bk. VIII, ch. 8).
65 Pieper, *Four Cardinal Virtues*, pp. 104–113.
66 Compare Pegis, *Basic Writings of Aquinas*, II, p. 461.
67 Del Vecchio, *Justice*, p. 148. See, also, Perelman, *The Idea of Justice* p. 60: "An imperfect [system of] justice, without charity, is no justice." Since all existing systems of justice are imperfect, they need to "draw fresh inspiration" from the more immediate and spontaneous values, the chief of which is charity.

3 THE RIGHTEOUSNESS OF GOD AND HUMAN JUSTICE

1 In *Exodus and Revolution* (New York: Basic Books, 1985), Michael Walzer explores the secular meaning of the Exodus event. For Walzer, the biblical narrative itself – a story of bondage, deliverance, covenant, and promised land – provides a paradigm for understanding the meaning and proper form of politics,

including revolutionary movements. His analysis of the secular meaning of the story is imaginative and incisive. Despite his attempt to bracket the theological basis of the account, however, the question remains whether such biblical symbols as the Exodus and the covenant can be adequately understood exclusively in secular terms.

2 Joseph L. Allen, *Love and Conflict: A Covenantal Model of Christian Ethics* (Nashville: Abingdon Press, 1984), pp. 18–19.

3 Gerhard von Rad, *Old Testament Theology*, 2 vols. (New York: Harper & Brothers, 1962–1965), 1, p. 134.

4 In Deuteronomy 5:2ff., the making of the covenant is located at Horeb.

5 For brief accounts of recent Old Testament studies on covenant, see Robert A. Oden, Jr., "The Place of Covenant in the Religion of Israel," in Patrick D. Miller, Jr., Paul D. Hanson, and S. Dean McBride (eds.), *Ancient Israelite Religion* (Philadelphia: Fortress Press, 1987), pp. 429–447; Ernest W. Nicholson, *God and His People: Covenant and Theology in the Old Testament* (Oxford: Clarendon Press, 1986), pp. 83–117. See also Brevard S. Childs, *The Book of Exodus: A Critical Theological Commentary* (Philadelphia: The Westminster Press, 1974), pp. 337–511.

6 *Decalogue* is the Greek translation of the Hebrew term.

7 See von Rad, *Old Testament Theology*, 1, p. 199.

8 Childs, *Book of Exodus*, p. 44.

9 Compare Walter Harrelson, *The Ten Commandments and Human Rights* (Philadelphia: Fortress Press, 1980).

10 J. J. Stamm, *The Ten Commandments in Recent Research*, translated with additions by M. E. Andrews (London: S. C. M. Press, Ltd., 1967), pp. 70–71; see also, pp. 113–114.

11 See Walther Eichrodt, *Man in the Old Testament* (Chicago: Alec R. Allenson, Inc., 1951), p. 21: "[T]he fundamental datum of Israel's view of life is that the individual is summoned to a responsibility which demands to be taken as absolute." As Hillers suggests, however, such responsibility is demanded not just of the individual; in the covenant at Sinai, the stress is upon "Israel's responsibilty" as a nation. Delbert R. Hillers, *Covenant: The History of a Biblical Idea* (Baltimore: The Johns Hopkins Press, 1969), p. 112.

12 Harrelson, *Ten Commandments*, p. 80. See also Martin Noth, *The Laws in the Pentateuch and Other Studies* (Philadelphia: Fortress Press, 1967), pp. 38ff.; J. Alberto Soggin; *Introduction to the Old Testament*, 3rd edn. (Louisville, Kentucky: Westminster/John Knox, 1989), pp. 164–175; Walther Zimmerli, *The Law and the Prophets* (Oxford: Basil Blackwell, 1965), pp. 31–45.

13 For this translation of v.11, see Childs, *Book of Exodus*, p. 442. The RSV reads: "she shall go out for nothing, without payment of money."

14 The best-known example of the latter is the Code of Hammurabi (ca. 2000–1700 BC). The Book of the Covenant probably comes from about 750–700 BC, although in its present setting – as noted above – it is included along with the Decalogue in the pact at Sinai.

15 See Soggin, *Introduction to Old Testament*, pp. 164–175, esp. 174–175; Childs, *Book of Exodus*, pp. 472–473.

16 Walther Eichrodt, *Theology of the Old Testament*, 2 vols. (Philadelphia: The Westminster Press, 1961), 1, p. 91.

17 Stamm, *Ten Commandments*, pp. 70–73, 113–114; E. W. Nicholson, *Deuteronomy and Tradition* (Oxford: Basil Blackwell, 1967), p. 70.

18 Jon D. Levenson, *Sinai and Zion: An Entry Into the Jewish Bible* (Minneapolis, Minnesota: Winston Press, 1985), p. 50.

19 Noth, *Laws in the Pentateuch*, pp. 18–20. See, also, Eichrodt, *Theology of the Old Testament*, 1, p. 90.

20 Noth, *Laws in the Pentateuch*, p. 35.

21 Eichrodt, *Theology of the Old Testament*, 1, p. 92.

22 Harrelson, *Ten Commandments*, p. 85.

23 It is generally agreed that the "book of the law" that Josiah used as the basis of his reform was Deuteronomy although probably not in its present form. Nicholson, *Deuteronomy and Tradition*, p. 16.

24 See also the laws related to the year of jubilee (Lev. 25).

25 Eichrodt, *Theology of the Old Testament*, 1, pp. 94–95.

26 Harrelson, *Ten Commandments*, p. 86.

27 See David Noel Freedman, "The Formation of the Canon of the Old Testament: The Selection and Identification of the Torah as the Supreme Authority of the Postexilic Community," in Edwin Brown Firmage, Bernard G. Weiss, and John W. Welch (eds.), *Religion and Law: Biblical-Judaic and Islamic Perspectives* (Winona Lake: Eisenbrauns, 1990), pp. 315–331.

28 Georg Fohrer, *Introduction to the Old Testament*, translated by David E. Green (Nashville: Abingdon Press, 1968), pp. 169–178. This early form of Deuteronomy is commonly called Proto-Deuteronomy.

29 *Ibid.*, p. 483.

30 See Gerhard von Rad, *The Message of the Prophets* (London: S. C. M. Press, Ltd., 1968), pp. 13–14; R. E. Clements, *Prophecy and Tradition* (Atlanta, Georgia: John Knox Press, 1975); Johannes Lindblom, *Prophecy in Ancient Israel* (Oxford: Blackwell, 1962), pp. 314–315; B.D.

Napier, "Prophet, Prophetism," *The Interpreter's Dictionary of the Bible*, vol. IV (Nashville: Abingdon Press, 1962), pp. 896–919, esp. pp. 901–903.

31 See Amos 9:10; Hos. 1:9; 4:6, 8, 12; 11:7; Is. 1:3; 3:12, 15; 5:13; 10:2, 24; 26:20; 32:13, 18; Mic. 1:9; 2:4, 8, 9; 3:3, 5; 6:3. See, also, Nicholson, *God and His People*, p. 206.

32 See James Barr, *Semantics and Biblical Language* (London: Oxford University Press, 1961), pp. 263–296. Use of the English term "election" is analogous to the theological use of the term "creation" to express an idea which is clearly present in certain biblical passages as a whole, even in the absence of the specific Hebrew word for "create." *Ibid*, pp. 281–282; compare p. 270. Compare, also, James Luther Mays, *Amos* (London: S. C. M. Press, Ltd., 1968), p. 7: "Amos never speaks directly of a covenant between Yahweh and Israel. But it must have been some form of the covenant tradition which lay behind and gave content to the relation implied in 'Israel my people.'" See, also, Lindblom, *Prophecy in Ancient Israel*, pp. 330–331.

33 Norman H. Snaith, *The Distinctive Ideas of the Old Testament* (New York: Schocken Books, 1964), pp. 51–78. See also Abraham J. Heschel, *The Prophets* (New York: Harper & Row, 1962), pp. 200–201.

34 *Tsedeq* means the moral order which God has established and which he upholds. Nicholson, *God and His People*, p. 206.

35 For this translation, see Heschel, *The Prophets*, p. 210.

36 Snaith, *Distinctive Ideas*, p. 59.

37 See Clements, *Prophecy and Tradition*, pp. 58–72.

38 See Stephen Charles Mott, *Biblical Ethics and Social Change* (New York: Oxford University Press, 1982), pp. 65–72.

39 See Fohrer, *Introduction to the Old Testament*, pp. 373, 402, 424–425; Heschel, *The Prophets*, pp. 60, 229; Norman K. Gottwald, *A Light to the Nations: An Introduction to the Old Testament* (New York: Harper & Brothers, 1959), pp. 302–303; 366–368.

40 Heschel, *The Prophets*, p. 213.

41 James L. Mays, "Justice: Perspectives from the Prophetic Tradition," in David L. Petersen (ed.), *Prophecy in Israel* (Philadelphia: Fortress Press, 1987), pp. 144–158, esp. p. 152.

42 *Ibid.*, p. 152.

43 For this translation, see *ibid.*, p. 151.

44 Paul Tillich, *Love, Power, and Justice* (New York: Oxford University Press, 1954), p. 64.

45 Mott, *Biblical Ethics*, p. 65.

46 Tillich, *Love, Power, and Justice*, p. 71.

4 JUSTICE IN THE PURITAN COVENANT TRADITION

1 On the sources of Puritan covenant theology in England, see Michael McGiffert, "Grace and Works: The Rise and Division of Covenant Divinity in Elizabethan Puritanism," *Harvard Theological Review* 75:4 (October, 1982), pp. 463–502. See, also, Leonard J. Trinterud, "The Origins of Puritanism," *Church History* 20:1 (March, 1951), pp. 37–57; Jens G. Møller, "The Beginnings of Puritan Covenant Theology," *Journal of Ecclesiastical History* 14 (1963), pp. 46–67; Richard L. Greaves, "The Origins and Early Development of English Covenant Thought," *Historian* 31 (1968), pp. 21–35; and Michael McGiffert, "Covenant, Crown, and Commons in Elizabethan Puritanism," *The Journal of British Studies* 20:1 (Fall, 1980), pp. 32–52.
2 John Calvin, *Institutes of the Christian Religion*, seventh American edition, 2 vols. (Philadelphia: Presbyterian Board of Christian Education, 1936), I, Bk.IV, ch. 20, sec. 31.
3 Trinterud, "The Origins of English Puritanism," pp. 37–57.
4 Compare Perry Miller, *The New England Mind: The Seventeenth Century* (New York: Macmillan Company, 1939), pp. 392–397.
5 In this sense "covenant" constitutes an important "root metaphor" for understanding our human existence in both its historical and its contemporary forms. On the meaning of root metaphors, see Stephen Popper, *World Hypotheses* (Berkeley: University of California Press, 1961).
6 On the relationship between Calvin and covenantal thought, see Ian Breward (ed.), *The Works of William Perkins* (Appleford, Abingdon, Berkshire, England: The Sutton Courtenay Press, 1970), pp. 90ff.; William K.B. Stoever, *"A Faire and Easie Way to Heaven": Covenant Theology and Antinomianism in Massachusetts* (Middletown, Connecticut: Wesleyan University Press, 1978); and Norman Pettit, *The Heart Prepared: Grace and Conversion in Puritan Spiritual Life* (New Haven: Yale University Press, 1966), esp. pp. 219–221.

For a more general discussion of the influence of Continental Protestantism upon Puritanism in England, see Pettit, *The Heart Prepared*; Michael Walzer, *The Revolution of the Saints: A Study in the Origins of Radical Politics* (Cambridge, Massachusetts: Harvard University Press, 1965); David Little, *Religion, Order, and Law: A Study in Pre-Revolutionary England* (New York: Harper & Row, 1969), pp. 250–259; and Everett H. Emerson, "Calvin and Covenant," *Church History* 25 (1956), pp. 136–144.
7 Walzer, *The Revolution of the Saints*, pp. 92–109. Compare Roland H.

152 *Notes to pages 57–60*

Bainton, "Congregationalism: From the Just War to the Crusades in the Puritan Revolution," *Andover Newton Theological Bulletin* 35:1–3 (1943).

8 Walzer, *The Revolution of the Saints*, pp. 302–306. On the relationship of covenant theology in New England to liberalism, see Miller, *The New England Mind: The Seventeenth Century*, p. 418; and Perry Miller, *The New England Mind: From Colony to Province* (Cambridge, Mass.: Harvard University Press, 1953), pp. 383–384. See also, James Hastings Nichols, *Democracy and the Churches* (Philadelphia: The Westminster Press, 1951). Nichols develops the thesis that liberal democracy was the creation of Puritanism in England in the 1640s and 1650s.

9 Walzer, *The Revolution of the Saints*, pp. 304–305.

10 David Zaret, *The Heavenly Contract: Ideology and Organization in Pre-Revolutionary Puritanism* (The University of Chicago Press, 1985), pp. 3, 24–60.

11 *Ibid.*, p. 4.

12., *Ibid.*, pp. 18, 163.

13 *Ibid.*, p. 164. In this connection, see M. M. Knappen, *Tudor Puritanism* (The University of Chicago Press, 1939). In sharp contrast to Zaret, Knappen describes individualism in sixteenth century Puritanism as "collectivist individualism." *Ibid.*, p. 348.

14 *Ibid.*, p. 4.

15 In the present work attention is focused primarily upon Perkins, Preston, Sibbes, Ames, and Baxter in England and upon Winthrop, Cotton, Ward, Mitchell, Willard, and Wise in New England. For a fuller description of the radical implications of covenantal thought, attention would need to be given to the Left-wing English sects; to the Army Debates, particularly the Putney Debates of 1647, over who should as a matter of justice participate in the civil covenant; and to the controversies of Roger Williams with Winthrop and John Cotton in New England over the limits of the political covenant. (I am particularly indebted to Professor David Little for his suggestions in this regard.) On the Putney Debates, see A. S. P. Woodhouse (ed.), *Puritanism and Liberty, Being the Army Debates (1647–9) from the Clarke Manuscripts with Supplementary Documents* (The University of Chicago Press, 1951), pp. 1–124. On Roger Williams' disputes with Winthrop and Cotton, see Perry Miller, *Roger Williams: His Contribution to the American Tradition* (Indianapolis: The Bobbs-Merrill Company, Inc., 1953); and Edmund S. Morgan, *Roger Williams: The Church and the State* (New York: Harcourt, Brace & World, Inc., 1967).

16 Calvin, *Institutes of the Christian Religion*, 1, pp. 465–466.

17 William Perkins, "A Golden Chain," in Ian Breward (ed.), *The Works of William Perkins*, pp. 210–212; John Preston, *The New Covenant, or The Saints' Portion. A Treatise Concerning the All Sufficiency of God, Man's Righteousness, and the Covenant of Grace*, The Eighth Edition corrected (London, 1634), pp. 316ff.; and Richard Sibbes, *The Faithful Covenanter*, in *Works of Richard Sibbes*, edited with Memoir by Alexander B. Grosart, 7 vols. (Edinburgh, 1862–64); reprinted (Edinburgh: The Banner of Truth Trust, 1973–83), VI, pp. 3–4.

18 Genesis 17:1–14.

19 Perkins, *ibid.*, pp. 213–218; Preston, *ibid.*, pp. 326ff. See also Sibbes, *ibid.* Sibbes extends the covenant of grace back to Adam after the Fall. The covenant which God made with Adam after the Fall replaces the first pact based upon works. The covenant of grace was renewed with Abraham and with Moses, and it was established in its New Testament form by the death of Christ.

20 Perkins, *ibid.*, pp. 210–211.

21 Preston, *ibid.*, pp. 315ff.

22 Sibbes, *ibid.*, p. 3.

23 William Ames, *Conscience with the Power and Cases Thereof. Divided into V Books*. Translated out of Latin into English, 1639, Book v, p. 107.

24 Ames, *ibid.*, pp. 102–109. See also Richard Baxter, *A Holy Commonwealth* (London, 1659), pp. 50–53. (An excellent new edition of *A Holy Commonwealth*, edited by William Lamont, was published by Cambridge University Press in 1994. While all of Baxter's "Theses" are included in this edition, some of his explanatory commentaries have been deleted. It is for this reason that the London, 1659, edition is cited throughout in the present essay.). For a discussion of natural law in Puritanism in the early 1600s, see John Eusden, *Puritans, Lawyers, and Politics in Early Seventeenth-Century England* (New Haven: Yale University Press, 1958), pp. 126ff. Eusden argues that Ames was exceptional among early Puritans in his appeal to natural law. Use of this idea subsequently became much more widespread, however, both among English and among American Puritans. On Ames' influence upon Puritanism generally but particularly in New England, see "Introduction" in William Ames, *The Marrow of Theology: Williams Ames 1576–1633*, translated from the third Latin edition, 1629, and edited by John D. Eusden (Boston: Pilgrim Press, 1968), pp. 1–11.

25 Miller, *The New England Mind: The Seventeenth Century*, p. 384.

26 See McGiffert, "Covenant, Crown, and Commons," *The Journal of British Studies* 20:1 (Fall, 1980), pp. 32–52; see esp. pp. 48–50.

27 William Perkins, *A Plain and Faithful Exposition Upon Two First Verses of the 2 Chapter of Zephaniah*, in Breward, *ibid.*, pp. 293–294.

28 McGiffert, *ibid.*, p. 48.

29 *Ibid.*, p. 50.

30 *Ibid.*, pp. 145–146.

31 Jerald C. Brauer, and B. A. Gerrish (eds.), *The Westminster Dictionary of Church History* (Philadelphia: The Westminster Press, 1971), p. 755. See also John Cunningham, *The Church History of Scotland: From the Commencement of the Christian Era to the Present Time*, 2 vols. 2nd edn., (Edinburgh, 1882), I, pp. 526–530.

32 Baxter, *A Holy Commonwealth*, pp. 458–459.

33 Edmund S. Morgan (ed.), *Puritan Political Ideas, 1558–1794* (Indianapolis: The Bobbs-Merrill Company, Inc., 1965), p. 139.

34 Miller, *The New England Mind: The Seventeenth Century*, pp. 448–449.

35 *Ibid.*, p. 448.

36 Perry Miller (ed.), *The American Puritans: Their Prose and Poetry* (Garden City: Doubleday & Company, Inc., Anchor Books, 1956), pp. 85–86.

37 *Ibid.*, p. 89.

38 Morgan, *Puritan Political Ideas*, p. 90.

39 *Ibid.*, pp. 92–93.

40. Aristotle, *The Nicomachean Ethics* (ed. J. E. C. Weldon, 1930), p. 138.

41 Compare Miller, *The New England Mind: The Seventeenth Century*, p. 483: "The great end toward which the theory aspired, the moral which the leaders worked to instill into the minds of the people, citizens, or inhabitants, was the principle of communal responsibility."

42 William Perkins, *The Whole Treatise of Cases of Conscience*, in Thomas F. Merrill (ed.), *William Perkins, 1558–1602: English Puritanist. His Pioneer Works on Casuistry: "A Discourse of Conscience" and "The Whole Treatise of Cases of Conscience"* (Nieuwkoop, Netherlands: B. De Graaf, 1966), pp. 79–240.

43 *Ibid.*, p. 163.

44 *Ibid.*, p. 164.

45 *Ibid.*

46 Ames, *Conscience*, Book III, p. 63.

47 *Ibid.*, p. 82.

48 Breward, *The Works of William Perkins*, p. 187.

49 Preston, *The New Covenant*, p. 217.

50 *Ibid.*, p. 390.

51 John Preston, *Sermons Preached Before His Majestie, and upon other speciall occasions* (London, 1634), pp. 111–112.

52 Ames, *Conscience*, Book V, p. 110. Ames considers this definition of virtue to be more adequate than the concept of justice as "a perpetual and constant intent of giving to every man his due." *Ibid.*, p. 109.

53. *Ibid.*, p. 130.
54 William Perkins, *A Treatise on the Vocations or Callings of Men*, in Breward, *The Works of William Perkins*, pp. 446–449.
55 Richard Baxter, *How to do Good to Many, or The Public Good is the Christian Life. Directions and Motives to it* (London, 1682), p. 12.
56 Baxter, *A Holy Commonwealth*, p. 14.
57 *Ibid.*, p. 59.
58 Jonathan Mitchell, "Nehemiah on the Wall," in Miller, *The American Puritans*, p. 109.
59 *Ibid.*, p. 111.
60 Breward, *The Works of William Perkins*, p. 483.
61 William Perkins, "Epiekeia, or a Treatise of Christian Equity, and Moderation," in Morgan, *Puritan Political Ideas*, pp. 59–73, esp. p. 60.
62 *Ibid.*, p. 61.
63 *Ibid.*, p. 62.
64 *Ibid.*, p. 66.
65 *Ibid.*, pp. 72–73.
66 Breward, *The Works of William Perkins*, pp. 479–480.
67 *Ibid.* Breward characterizes Perkins' treatment of conscience as "a modified Thomist position." *Ibid.*, p. 63.
68 *Ibid.*, p. 480. Perkins' distinction between the extremity of the law and the mitigation of the law corresponds closely to Calvin's distinction between the two laws of equity in relation to the poor. "The first law of fair-dealing," Calvin writes, "is that no one is to lay claim to another's property, but use only what he can rightfully call his own. The second is that no one is to swallow what belongs to him like a whirlpool, but he is to be kindly toward his neighbors and lighten their want by his abundance": John Calvin, *Commentary on the Second Epistle to the Thessalonians*, in *Calvin's Commentaries on The Epistles of Paul the Apostle to the Romans and to the Thessalonians*, translated by Ross Mackenzie and edited by David W. Torrance and Thomas F. Torrance (Edinburgh: Oliver and Boyd, 1960), p. 420. See also Calvin, *Institutes*, II, pp. 787–791. "Equity, being natural, is the same to all mankind, and consequently all laws, on every subject, ought to have the same equity for their end. Particular enactments and regulations, being connected with circumstances, and partly dependent upon them, may be different in different cases without any impropriety, provided they are all equally directed to the same object of equity ... This equity, therefore, must alone be the scope, and rule, and end, of all laws": *Ibid.*, p. 789. The idea of equity was firmly rooted in Calvin and, through him and the Puritans, in the Reformed tradition.

69 Ames, *Conscience*, Book v, p. 111.
70 Morgan, *Puritan Political Ideas*, p. 138.
71 *Ibid.*, pp. 153–155.
72 *Ibid.*, p. 136.
73 Miller, *The American Puritans*, p. 109.
74 Perry Miller, "The Marrow of Puritan Divinity," *Publications of the Colonial Society of Massachusetts* xxxii (*Transactions 1933–37*), pp. 294–300. Cf. Miller, *The New England Mind: The Seventeenth Century*, pp. 111–206.
75 Samuel Willard, "The Character of a Good Ruler," in Perry Miller and Thomas H. Johnson (eds)., *The Puritans* (New York: American Book Company, 1938), p. 252. See also T. H. Breen, *The Character of the Good Ruler: A Study of Puritan Political Ideas in New England, 1630–1730* (New Haven: Yale University Press, 1970).
76 Morgan, *Puritan Political Ideas*, p. 60.
77 The original draft of this document, written by John Cotton, subsequently became the basic code of the New Haven Colony. A later draft, which was adopted by the Colony of Massachusetts, was written by Nathaniel Ward. *Ibid.*, pp. 177–178.
78 *Ibid.*, p. 179.
79 Miller, *The New England Mind: The Seventeenth Century*, pp. 439–440.
80 See Morgan, *Puritan Political Ideas*, pp. xl–xlvii. Compare Arthur H. Buffinton, "The Massachusetts Experiment of 1630," *Publications of the Colonial Society of Massachusetts* xxxii (*Transactions 1933–37*), pp. 308–320.
81 Edmund S. Morgan, *The Puritan Dilemma: The Story of John Winthrop* (Boston: Little, Brown and Company, 1958), pp. 84ff., esp. p. 91.
82 *Ibid.*, p. 93.
83 According to John Wise, the principles of natural liberty, equity, equality, and self-preservation rest fundamentally upon reason. "Revelation," Wise declared, "is nature's law in a fairer and brighter edition." John Wise, *A Vindication of the Government of the New England Churches, and the Churches' Quarrel Espoused; or, a Reply to Certain Proposals* (Boston: Congregational Board of Publications, 1860), pp. 27–28.
84 Morgan, *Puritan Political Ideas*, p. xli.
85 See John Locke, *Two Treatises of Government*, ed. Peter Laslett (Cambridge University Press, 2nd edn., 1967), p. 286. The reference is to the Second Treatise entitled *An Essay Concerning the True Original, Extent, and End of Civil Government*, chapter 1, section 3.
86 Compare John Dunn, *Locke* (Oxford University Press, 1984), chapter 2, "The Politics of Trust." "At the center of Locke's conception of government ... was the idea of trust." *Ibid.*, p. 52.

5 JOHN LOCKE: JUSTICE AND THE SOCIAL COMPACT

1 John Dunn, *The Political Thought of John Locke* (Cambridge University Press, 1969), pp. ix–xii.

2 James Tully, *A Discourse on Property: John Locke and His Adversaries* (Cambridge University Press, 1980), p. 36; Richard Ashcraft, *Locke's Two Treatises of Government* (London: Allen E. Unwin, 1987), pp. 304–305; John Colman, *John Locke's Moral Philosophy* (Edinburgh University Press, 1983). Tully, for example, writes: "Man is ... dependent on his maker for being brought into being and for his continuing existence. Locke's political philosophy hinges on this one-way dependency relation between God and man, and from which man's natural obligations follow ..."

3 Peter Laslett (ed.), *Two Treatises of Government*, 2nd edn. (Cambridge University Press, 1967), pp. 55–61; compare p. 31.

4 Tully, *A Discourse on Property*, pp. 53–176; compare Laslett, *Two Treatises*, pp. 100–106.

5 Ashcraft, *Locke's Two Treatises*, p. 305. See, also, Richard Ashcraft, *Revolutionary Politics and Locke's Two Treatises of Government* (Princeton University Press, 1986); Laslett, *Two Treatises*, pp. 21–44.

6 W. von Leyden (ed.), *John Locke: Essays on the Law of Nature* (Oxford: The Clarendon Press, 1954), pp. 21–30. See also Philip Abrams (ed.), *John Locke: Two Tracts on Government* (Cambridge University Press, 1967), pp. 3–27.

7 Dunn, *The Political Thought*, pp. 24–26.

8 On the tension between theological voluntarism and rationalism in Locke's ethical theory, see von Leyden, *John Locke*, pp. 51–58; Colman, *Locke's Moral Philosophy*, pp. 32–50; Dunn, *The Political Thought*, pp. 187–199; and David Little, "Natural Rights and Human Rights: The International Imperative," in Robert P. Davidow (ed.), *Natural Rights and Natural Law: The Legacy of George Mason* (Fairfax, Virginia: George Mason University Press), 1986, pp. 67–122, esp. pp. 115–116. On the whole Locke seems to have been a theological voluntarist because he held that the moral right – the right and the good – is dependent upon the will of God. In contrast, ethical rationalism holds that moral distinctions between good and evil do not depend upon God, for he can neither create nor change them. See Colman, *Locke's Moral Philosophy*, pp. 31–50.

9 Peter H. Nidditch (ed.), *John Locke: An Essay on Human Understanding* (Oxford: The Clarendon Press, 1975), bk. III. xi. 15–16; compare bk. IV. iii. 18.

10 John Locke, *The Reasonableness of Christianity, as delivered in the Scriptures,*

in *The Works of John Locke, in Nine Volumes*, 12th edn. (London, 1824), VI, pp. 138–158. As Colman suggests, however, such a turn did not represent a repudiation of his long-standing conviction that morality – like mathematics – could be rationally demonstrated; rather, it represented a postponement of the latter project in order to provide a more immediate and certain account of morality than was presently available on the basis of reason alone. Colman, *Locke's Moral Philosophy*, pp. 138–140. See also, Samuel C. Pearson, Jr., "The Religion of John Locke and the Character of his Thought," in Richard Ashcraft (ed.), *John Locke: Critical Assessments*, 4 vols. (London: Routledge, 1991), II, pp. 133–150.

11 All citations of *Two Treatises of Government* in the text refer to the Laslett edition (Cambridge, 1967). Citations include the number of the Treatise together with the relevant sections of the latter.

12 The Exclusion Crisis (1679–1681) was precipitated by the Whigs' attempt to exclude James, Duke of York, from succession to the English throne. The Whigs viewed the prospect of James' accession as a threat of popery and the establishment of an arbitrary monarchy. The *Two Treatises* may perhaps be best understood as "a revolutionary and distinctively rationalist contribution to the Exclusion Crisis" without being intended specifically as an "Exclusion tract": Tully, *A Discourse on Property*, p. 54; cf. Dunn, *The Political Thought*, pp. 51–52; contrast Laslett, *Two Treatises*, p. 61.

13 On the setting and dating of *Two Treatises*, see Dunn, *The Political Thought*, pp. 43–57; Tully, *A Discourse on Property*, pp. 53–55; Laslett, *Two Treatises*, pp. 45–66.

14 Laslett, *Two Treatises*, p. 155. The citation is taken from the Preface to *Two Treatises*. Locke's reference is to William III (1687–1702).

15 *Ibid.*, p. 82.

16 Tully, *A Discourse on Property*, p. 63; cf. Dunn, *The Political Thought*, p. 218. Contrast Leo Strauss, *Natural Right and History* (University of Chicago Press, 1953), p. 248. Strauss interprets Locke as a natural rights rather than a natural law theorist. He writes (p.227): "the right of nature is more fundamental [for Locke] than the law of nature and is the foundation of the law of nature." For a fuller treatment of natural law in Locke, see W. von Leyden, "John Locke and Natural Law," in Ashcraft, *John Locke: Critical Assessments*, II, pp. 1–129.

17 Tully, *A Discourse on Property*, p. 46.

18 Locke also calls the preservation of society "the first and fundamental natural law" [II.134]. Whether Locke intends this as a second law of nature or only as a special instance of the general obligation to preserve oneself and the rest of mankind – addressed this time to

the legislature – is unclear. In either case, however, the duty to preserve society is grounded in the law of nature.

19 Tully, *A Discourse on Property*, pp. 49–50.
20 Elsewhere Locke lists these rights in a number of varying forms: life, health, liberty, and possessions (ii.6); life, liberty, health, limb, or goods (ii.6); "lives, liberties, and estates" (ii.123; 222); "lives, liberties, or fortunes" (ii.221).
21 Tully, *A Discourse on Property*, pp. 62–63.
22 Laslett, *Two Treatises*, pp. 101; 341; 368–369. Richard Baxter similarly uses the term "property" to refer to the property which people have in their lives, liberties, and material possessions or acquisitions. Laslett, *Two Treatises*, pp. 101; 101n.; 305n.
23 Locke acknowledges that "children are not born in this full state of equality" though they are intended to grow into it as they increase in age and reason (ii.55).
24 Laslett, *Two Treatises*, p. 75.
25 Dunn, *The Political Thought*, p. 106.
26 In *Two Treatises* (ii.101) Locke also includes "love" as well as the "want of society" among the qualities which predispose man in the state of nature to enter into social groups.
27 For Locke, the fall of humanity was caused by the introduction of money. The latter gave rise to covetousness, ambition, and pride, thus greatly compounding the inconveniences of the state of nature and creating a further necessity for man to enter into civil society. See Tully, *A Discourse on Property*, p. 147; Dunn, *The Political Thought*, p. 205n. Locke's account of the fall is ambiguous, however. Theologically, the latter refers to the loss of humanity's original innocence, not to a subsequent worsening of its plight. It is not clear that Locke views humanity before the advent of money as either innocent or sinless. See, also, Colman, *Locke's Moral Philosophy*, pp. 192–193.
28 See Laslett, *Two Treatises*, p. 112. In *Two Treatises* "the word contract does not occur more than about ten times … and it is hardly ever applied to political matters at all." The term "contract" is generally applied to legal and quasi-legal agreements such as marriage or property arrangements. "Compact" and "agreement" are more general than "contract"; moreover, these are also "further removed from the language of law."
29 *Ibid.*, pp. 112–113.
30 The legislative is "only a fiduciary power to act for certain ends" (*Two Treatises*, ii.149). Similarly, the executive power is "a fiduciary trust" (ii.156).
31 Ashcraft, *Locke's Two Treatises*, p. 221.
32 See John Dunn, "Justice and the Interpretation of Locke's Political

Theory," *Political Studies* 16:1 (1968), pp. 68–87; Carl Friedrich and John W. Chapman (eds.), *Nomos IV. Justice* (New York: Atherton Press, 1963), esp. ch.12, Richard H. Cox, "Justice as the Basis of Political Order in Locke," and ch.13, Raymond Polin, "Justice in Locke's Philosophy"; Colman, *Locke's Moral Philosophy*, pp. 194–201. In contrast to his completed works, justice is the primary moral notion which he examines in an unfinished paper on "Morality": Colman, p. 194.

33 Compare Tully, *A Discourse on Property*, p. 131: "The priority of natural law renders all rights as means to this end [i.e., God's purpose], and therefore Locke's account is a *limited rights theory.*" (Italics added.)

34 Abrams, *John Locke*, pp. 231–232.

35 Dunn, "Justice and the Interpretation of Locke's Political Theory," p. 78.

36 Von Leyden, *John Locke*, p. 169.

37 *Ibid.*, p. 213.

38 Dunn, "Justice and the Interpretation of Locke's Political Theory," pp. 76–77. Locke refutes the claim that justice – or rightness – is based either upon personal interest or upon utility. "The rightness of an action does not depend upon its utility; on the contrary, its utility is a result of its rightness": von Leyden, *John Locke*, p. 215.

39 Dunn, "Justice and the Interpretation of Locke's Political Theory," pp. 78–79. See John Locke, *Essay on Toleration* (1667), in H. R. Fox Bourne, *The Life of John Locke*, 2 vols. (New York: Harper & Brothers, 1876), 1, pp. 174–194.

40 Benjamin Rand (ed.), *An Essay Concerning the Understanding, Knowledge, Opinion, and Assent by John Locke* (Cambridge, Mass.: Harvard University Press, 1931), pp. 291–306. This is a copy of the original draft of Locke's *Essay Concerning Human Understanding*, dating from 1671.

41 *Ibid.*, pp. 302–303; 306.

42 Tully, *A Discourse on Property*, pp. 79; 112.

43 For two radically different interpretations of Locke's account of property in political society, see Tully, *ibid.*, pp. 157–176, and Neal Wood, *John Locke and Agrarian Capitalism* (Berkeley: University of California, 1984), pp. 72–92. In contrast to Tully's egalitarian interpretation, Wood argues that Locke was "a theorist of developing agrarian capitalism and, in a broader sense, a pioneer of the spirit of capitalism": Wood, *ibid.*, p. 114.

44 Colman, *Locke's Moral Philosophy*, p. 193.

45 *Ibid.*, pp. 121–124; 169–170. "A property in something is more extensive than a traditional use right ... Locke's 'property in' ... is the right to use and enjoy God's property for God's purpose. The

kind of exclusive right which Locke develops is the uniquely English concept of *use* which a trustee is said to have in another's property.": *ibid.*, p. 122.

46 On the role of distributive justice in Locke, see Dunn, "Justice and the Interpretation of Locke's Political Theory," p. 76; Tully, *A Discourse on Property*, pp. 90–91; 162–170.

47 Some commentators suggest that Locke became more conservative in his views concerning property and trade after his appointment as Commissioner of Appeals (1689) and commissioner of trade and plantations (1696). See Bourne, *The Life of John Locke*, II, pp. 174; 350.

48 Von Leyden, *John Locke*, p. 205.

49 *Ibid.*, p. 169.

50 On the relation of justice to other virtues, including charity, in Locke, see Colman, *John Locke's Moral Philosophy*, pp. 194–205. See also John C. Winfrey, "Charity versus Justice in Locke's Theory of Property," in Ashcraft, *Critical Assessments*, III, pp. 385–401.

51 For Locke, the state of nature was "a state of peace, good will, mutual assistance, and preservation." *Two Treatises*, II.19.

52 Colman, *Locke's Moral Philosophy*, p. 195. Spelling and punctuation have been changed.

53 *Ibid.*, p. 199.

54 *Ibid.* The quotation is taken from *Conduct of the Understanding*.

55 Locke, *The Reasonableness of Christianity*, pp. 138–140.

56 John Locke, "A Paraphrase and Notes on Saint Paul's First Epistle to the Corinthians," in Locke, *Works*, VII, pp. 170–171.

57 Tully, *A Discourse on Property*, pp. 175–176. Throughout this paragraph I am indebted to Tully, who first called Locke's treatment of liberality in relation to property to my attention and suggested the enhancement of Locke's concept of enjoyment to include generosity.

58 See John Locke, *Some Thoughts Concerning Education* in Locke, *Works*, VIII, pp. 100–101.

59 It should be noted, however, that Locke did not develop this idea. See Tully, *A Discourse on Property*, pp. 175–176; Nathan Tarcov, *Locke's Education for Liberty* (The University of Chicago Press, 1984), pp. 145–148. Compare Colman, *Locke's Moral Philosophy*, p. 204; Dunn, "Justice and the Interpretation of Locke's Political Theory," p. 83.

60 For an excellent treatment of the concept of trust in Locke, see Laslett, *Two Treatises*, pp. 97–120. See, also, Dunn, *The Political Thought*, pp. 154–164; John Dunn, *Locke* (Oxford University Press, 1984), pp. 22–59. For a helpful discussion of the origin and development of the distinctively English concept of trust – including its uses by Milton, Cromwell, and Baxter – see J. W. Gough, *John Locke's Political Philosophy* (Oxford University Press, 1973), pp. 154–192.

Gough writes: "One result of this [development] in the political sphere has been that whereas the thought of continental thinkers was often forced into contractual terms, English thinkers had in the trust concept a fruitful alternative to the idea of contract": *ibid.,* p. 189.

61 Laslett, *Two Treatises*, pp. 97–108.
62 Compare John Dunn, "The Concept of Trust in the Politics of John Locke," in Richard Rorty, J. B. Schneewind and Quentin Skinner (eds.), *Philosophy and History* (Cambridge University Press, 1984), p. 297.

6 THE AMERICAN REPUBLIC – A CASE STUDY: CIVIC VIRTUE AND THE PUBLIC GOOD

1 See Donald S. Lutz, *The Origins of American Constitutionalism* (Baton Rouge: Louisiana State University Press, 1988), pp. 5–12; 166.
2 Bernard Bailyn, *The Ideological Origins of the American Revolution* (Cambridge, Massachusetts: Harvard University Press, 1967), pp. 22–54. See also Gordon S. Wood, *The Creation of the American Republic 1776–1787* (Chapel Hill: The University of North Carolina Press, 1969), pp. 1–124, esp. pp. 3–17; Stephen L. Schechter (ed.), *Roots of the Republic: American Founding Documents Interpreted*, Richard B. Bernstein and Donald S. Lutz, contributing editors (Madison, Wisconsin: Madison House, 1990).
3 Bailyn, *The Ideological Origins*, pp. 33–54; Wood, *The Creation of the American Republic*, pp. 14–17.
4 Wood, *ibid.,* pp. 46–124. See, also, J. G. A. Pocock, *The Machiavellian Moment: Florentine Political Thought and the Atlantic Republican Tradition* (Princeton University Press, 1975); and Pocock, "Between Gog and Magog: The Republican Thesis and the *Ideologia Americana*," *The Journal of the History of Ideas* 48:2 (April–June, 1987), pp. 325–346.
5 Pocock, "Between Gog and Magog," p. 345.
6 Bailyn, *The Ideological Origins*, p. 32.
7 Lutz, *The Origins of American Constitutionalism*, pp. 21–22.
8 Although modern bills of rights, including that contained in the national Constitution, have become much more legalistic than their pre-Revolutionary counterparts, the former are directly descended from the latter.
9 Lutz, *The Origins of American Constitutionalism*, pp. 32–34.
10 For a helpful analysis of three types of covenants in Puritanism – social, political, and ecclesiastical – see John Witte, Jr., "How to Govern a City on a Hill: The Early Puritan Contribution to

American Constitutionalism," *Emory Law Journal*, 39:1 (Winter 1990), pp. 41–64, see esp., pp. 44–54.

11 See H. Richard Niebuhr, *The Kingdom of God in America* (New York: Harper & Brothers, 1937).

12 Schechter, *Roots of the Republic*, pp. 22–23.

13 John Winthrop, "A Model of Christian Charity," in Perry Miller (ed.), *The American Puritans: Their Prose and Poetry* (New York: Doubleday & Company, Inc., Anchor Books, 1956), pp. 78–84.

14 Lutz identified more than 100 documents similar in form to the Mayflower Compact written by the colonists in the 1600s: Schechter, *Roots of the Republic*, p. 19.

15 The Pilgrim Code (1636), for example, was both a covenant and a constitution; similarly, the Fundamental Orders of Connecticut (1639) was a compact and also a constitution: Lutz, *The Origins of American Constitutionalism*, p. 27; Schechter, *Roots of the Republic*, p. 26.

16 Donald S. Lutz, "Religious Dimensions in the Development of American Constitutionalism," *Emory Law Journal* 39:1 (Winter, 1990), pp. 21–40; esp. pp. 35–40.

17 The Declaration, the Articles of Confederation, and the state constitutions comprised the first American constitutional system. It was replaced in 1787–1791 by the present system: Schechter, *Roots of the Republic*, pp. 13–14.

18 Lutz, "Religious Dimensions", p. 38. Compare 3">ibid., p. 40: "We are still effectively a covenanted people."

19 Wood, *The Creation of the American Republic*, p. 602.

20 *Ibid.*, pp. 593–600.

21 See Melvin Richter, *The Political Theory of Montesquieu* (Cambridge University Press, 1977), pp. 188–196. In book III of *The Spirit of the Laws* (1748), Montesquieu describes three principles which, he believed, distinguished three forms of government – democracy, aristocracy, and monarchy. The principle of democracy is virtue; the principle of aristocracy is moderation; and the principle of monarchy is honor. Montesquieu does not mean that these principles do in fact exist in any particular form of government. His point is that each of these forms of government ought to be actuated by its respective principle; otherwise it will be "imperfect."

22 See Pocock, *The Machiavellian Moment*, pp. viii–ix; 83ff.; 219–271.

23 *Ibid.*, p. 545. On the influence of republicanism in America during this period, see *ibid.*, pp. 506–552, chapter xv: "The Americanization of Virtue."

24 See Lutz, *The Origins of American Constitutionalism*, pp. 81–83.

25 Schechter, *Roots of the Republic*, pp. 291–334, chapter xv: "*The Federalist* on Federalism"; see esp., p. 297.

26 Ralph Ketcham, "Antifederalist Essays and Speeches 1787–1788," in Schechter, *Roots of the Republic*, p. 384.

27 See Schechter, *Roots of the Republic*, pp. 271–276; Lutz, *The Origins of American Constitutionalism*, pp. 92–95.

28 The Tenth Amendment, which was later added as part of the Bill of Rights, further specified that those powers which were neither delegated to the United States by the Constitution nor prohibited to the states by the latter were reserved to the states or to the people.

29 See James Madison, *The Federalist No. 10*, in Schechter, *Roots of the Republic*, pp. 309–316; see, esp., p. 316.

30 Wood, *The Creation of the American Republic*, p. 613. The phrase is borrowed from Thomas Pownall.

31 This Amendment constitutes the first right protected under the Bill of Rights. Originally understood as pertaining only to Congress, this provision has subsequently (1949) been held applicable to the states under the "due process" clause of the Fourteenth Amendment. See Wilber G. Katz, "Religion and Law in America," in James Ward Smith and A. Leland Jamison (eds.), *Religious Perspectives in American Culture* (Princeton University Press, 1961), pp. 53–80. Established churches continued to exist in a number of the states on into the next century. Massachusetts was the last state to abolish its established church (1833).

32 *Ibid.*, p. 54.

33 For Katz religious liberty means governmental neutrality toward religion. In contrast to Katz, Anson Phelps Stokes describes church-state relations in the United States as a combination of the principle of separation with an attitude of governmental "friendliness" toward the churches. Anson Phelps Stokes, *Church and State in the United States*, 3 vols. (New York: Harper & Brothers, 1950), III, p. 694.

34 Harold J. Berman, *The Interaction of Law and Religion* (Nashville: Abingdon Press, 1974), p. 11.

35 Alexis de Tocqueville, *Democracy in America*, 2 vols. (London, 1838), II, pp. 146–147.

36 Pocock, *The Machiavellian Moment*, pp. 462; 526–552.

37 Abraham Lincoln, "The Gettysburg Address."

7 COVENANT, JUSTICE, AND LAW

1 Edmund S. Morgan, *The Puritan Dilemma: The Story of John Winthrop* (Boston: Little, Brown, & Company, 1958), p. 93.

2 Leonard J. Trinterud, "The Origins of Puritanism," *Church History* 20 (1951), pp. 37–57; see esp., p. 48. The covenant of grace was a covenant of redemption since it was instituted after the Fall (post-

lapsarian). The covenant of works, on the other hand, was a covenant of creation since it was given prior to the Fall (prelapsarian).

3 See H. Richard Niebuhr, *The Kingdom of God in America* (New York: Harper & Brothers, 1937).

4 Donald Lutz, "The Declaration of Independence, 1776. Commentary by Donald S. Lutz," in Stephen L. Schechter (ed.), *Roots of the Republic* (Madison, Wisconsin: Madison House, 1990), pp. 139–140.

5 Preamble to The United States Constitution. See Schechter, *Roots*, p. 277.

6 Alasdair MacIntyre, *After Virtue* (Notre Dame, Indiana: University of Notre Dame Press, 1981), pp. 195, 203.

7 James M. Gustafson's theocentric ethics contains a broad basis for community grounded in creation and also for an affirmation of pluralism. In these respects he reflects the influence of the Reformed tradition. See James M. Gustafson, *Ethics from a Theocentric Perspective* (The University of Chicago Press, 1981–1984). See, esp., vol. 1, ch. 4: "A Preference for the Reformed Tradition," pp. 157–193.

8 H. Richard Niebuhr, *The Responsible Self* (New York: Harper & Row, 1963).

9 H. Richard Niebuhr, *Radical Monotheism and Western Culture with Supplementary Essays* (New York: Harper & Brothers, 1960), p. 111. Italics in original.

10 Niebuhr, *The Responsible Self*, p. 126.

11 See, for example, James M. Gustafson, *Can Ethics be Christian?* (The University of Chicago Press, 1975), pp. 149–150; 156–157.

12 Niebuhr writes: "Yet something like that freedom of which teleological and deontological thinkers speak in their different ways also comes into appearance when we analyze ourselves as responsive, time-full beings. The question of freedom arises in this connection as the question of the self's ability in its present to change its past and future and to achieve or receive a new understanding of its ultimate historical context. If these two modifications are possible, then reinterpretation of present action upon the self must result, and a new kind of reaction, a response that fits into another lifetime and another history, can and will take place": *The Responsible Self*, p. 101. For a fuller development of Niebuhr's concept of freedom, see *ibid.*, pp. 90–126: ch. 3, "The Responsible Self in Time and History" and ch. 4, "Responsibility in Absolute Dependence."

13 *Ibid.*, pp. 60–61.

14 H. Richard Niebuhr, "The Center of Value," in *Radical Monotheism*, pp. 100–113; see esp., p. 103.

15 See Gustafson, *Ethics from a Theocentric Perspective*, 1, pp. 327–342. See, also, Gustafson, "Moral Discernment in the Christian Life," in Gene H. Outka and Paul Ramsey (eds.), *Norm and Context in Christian Ethics* (New York: Scribner's, 1968), pp. 17–36.
16 Niebuhr, *The Responsible Self*, pp. 60–65.
17 Niebuhr, *Radical Monotheism*, p. 41.
18 See H. Richard Niebuhr, "The Idea of Covenant and American Democracy," *Church History* 23 (1954), pp. 126–135; Niebuhr, *Radical Monotheism*, pp. 38–48; Milner S. Ball, *The Promise of American Law: A Theological, Humanistic View of Legal Process* (Athens, Georgia: The University of Georgia Press, 1981); Robert N. Bellah, *The Broken Covenant: American Civil Religion in Time of Trial* (New York: Seabury, 1975); Paul Ramsey, *Basic Christian Ethics* (New York: Charles Scribner's Sons, 1950).
19 John Calvin, *Institutes of the Christian Religion*, seventh American edn., 2 vols. (Philadelphia: Presbyterian Board of Christian Education, 1936), II, p. 804.
20 See Baxter, *A Holy Commonwealth*, pp. 180–183; 211. See also ch. 12, "Of due Obedience to Rulers, and of Resistance," esp. pp. 375–379, 429–450.
21 Hugo Grotius, *De jure belli ac pacis*, (Paris, 1625).
22 Thomas Hobbes, *Leviathan; or The Matter, Form, and Power of a Commonwealth Ecclesiastical and Civil*, in Edwin A. Burtt (ed.), *The English Philosophers from Bacon to Mill* (New York: The Modern Library, 1939). See esp., *Leviathan*, ch. XIV, "Of the First and Second Natural Laws, and of Contracts."
23 John Locke, *Two Treatises of Government*, ed. Peter Laslett, 2 vols. (Cambridge University Press, 2nd. edn., 1967), II, p. 19.
24 Compare Robert N. Bellah, Richard Madsen, William M. Sullivan, Ann Swidler, and Steven M. Tipton, *The Good Society* (New York: Alfred Knopf, 1991), pp. 264–270.
25 See James W. Nickel, *Making Sense of Human Rights: Philosophical Reflections on the Universal Declaration of Human Rights* (Berkeley: University of California Press, 1987). See esp., pp. 181–186, " Universal Declaration of Human Rights, 1948"; cf. pp. 211–229, "International Covenant on Civil and Political Rights, 1966"; and pp. 230–240, "International Covenant on Economic, Social, and Cultural Rights, 1966." In each case, the Preamble declares that "recognition of the inherent dignity and of the equal and inalienable rights of all members of the human family is the foundation of freedom, justice, and peace in the world."
26 David Little makes a similar observation about the Bill of Rights in the United States Constitution in contrast to the Declaration

of Independence: "The United States Constitution, of course,
enumerates many of the civil and political rights that were later
incorporated into international human-rights instruments, but it
is shorn of any ringing, vindicating phrases that might reveal its
intellectual and spiritual sources. Conversely, the Declaration of
Independence contains eloquent references to the grounds of the
American experiment": David Little, "Natural Rights and
Human Rights: The International Imperative," in Robert P.
Davidow (ed.), *Natural Rights and Natural Law: The Legacy of George
Mason* (Fairfax, Virginia: George Mason University Press, 1986),
p. 67.

27 See R. Bruce Douglass, Gerald M. Mara, and Henry Richardson
(eds.), *Liberalism and the Good* (New York: Routledge, 1990); see esp.,
pp. 148–166, 253–280. On the need of "political space" for public
discourse, see Sheldon Wolin, *Politics and Vision: Continuity and
Innovation in Western Political Thought* (Boston: Little, Brown, 1960),
p. 16. See also, Stephen L. Carter, *The Culture of Disbelief: How
American Law and Politics Trivialize Religious Devotion* (New York: Basic
Books, 1993).

28 On the relationship of covenant to rights in Christian ethics, see
Joseph L. Allen, *Love and Conflict: A Covenantal Model of Christian Ethics*
(Nashville: Abingdon Press, 1984); see also, Kieran Cronin, *Rights
and Christian Ethics* (Cambridge University Press, 1992). On the
covenantal model of Christian ethics generally, see Paul Ramsey,
Basic Christian Ethics (New York: Charles Scribner's Sons, 1950), esp.
pp. 367–388, and *The Patient as Person* (New Haven: Yale University
Press, 1970); and Niebuhr, *Radical Monotheism*, pp. 38–48.

29 Puritans such as Perkins and Baxter also spoke of "the common
good." See William Perkins, *A Treatise on the Vocations or Callings of
Men*, in Ian Breward (ed.), *The Works of William Perkins*, pp. 446–449;
Baxter, *A Holy Commonwealth*, pp. 14; 59.

30 David Hollenbach, *Justice, Peace, and Human Rights: American Catholic
Social Ethics in a Pluralistic World* (New York: Crossroad, 1988),
pp. 186–187. Traditional teachings regarding such matters as private
property, political inequality, the illegitimacy of contraception, and
the subordination of woman to man were all justified "primarily by
nontheological appeals to the law of nature." Theological and
biblical appeals were used secondarily to buttress those nontheological arguments. See also, pp. 16–33. Hollenbach calls the law of
nature " a form of natural-law theory."

31 See David Hollenbach, *Claims in Conflict: Retrieving and Preserving the
Catholic Human Rights Tradition* (New York: Paulist Press, 1979),
pp. 41–106. See also, Todd David Whittemore "Immunity or

Empowerment? John Courtney Murray and the Question of Religious Liberty," *The Journal of Religious Ethics* 21/2 (Fall, 1993), pp. 247–273, esp. pp. 260–263.

32 Hollenbach, *Justice, Peace, and Human Rights*, p. 187. See also, Joseph Gremillion, *The Gospel of Peace and Justice: Catholic Social Teaching Since Pope John* (Maryknoll, New York: Orbis Books, 1976), esp. pp. 7–10, 531–567.

33 See David Hollenbach, "The Common Good Revisited," *Theological Studies* 50 (1989), pp. 70–94, esp. p. 88. See also, National Conference of Catholic Bishops, *Economic Justice for All: Pastoral Letter on Catholic Social Teaching and the U.S. Economy* (Washington, D.C.: United States Catholic Conference, 1986), pars. 79–84.

34 Michael Walzer, *Spheres of Justice: A Defense of Pluralism and Equality* (New York: Basic Books, 1983).

35 See William F. May, *The Physician's Covenant: Images of the Healer in Medical Ethics* (Philadelphia: The Westminster Press, 1983).

36 Melvin Konner, *Dear America, A Concerned Doctor Wants You to Know the Truth About Health Reform* (Reading, Massachusetts: Addison-Wesley Publishing Company, 1993), p. 92.

37 See Paul Starr, *The Social Transformation of American Medicine* (New York: Basic Books, 1982).

38 President's Commission for the Study of Ethical Problems in Medicine and Biomedical and Behavioral Research, *Summing Up: Final Report on Studies of the Ethical and Legal Problems in Medicine and Biomedical and Behavioral Research*, 1983, p. 29.

39 Compare Hessel Bouma III, Douglas Diekema, Edward Longerak, Theodore Rottman, and Allen Verhey, *Christian Faith, Health and Medical Practice* (Grand Rapids, Michigan: William B. Eerdmans, 1989), pp. 51–52.

40 Calvin, *Institutes of the Christian Religion*, ii, p. 775.

41 See Michael Walzer, *The Revolution of the Saints: A Study in the Origins of Radical Politics* (Cambridge, Massachusetts: Harvard University Press, 1965).

42 Compare James Madison: "Justice is the end of government. It is the end of civil society." Quoted in Gordon S. Wood, *The Creation of the American Republic 1776–1787* (Chapel Hill: The University of North Carolina Press, 1969), p. 609.

43 In this connection, see Gary J. Dorrien, *Reconstructing the Common Good: Theology and the Social Order* (Maryknoll, New York: Orbis Books, 1990).

44 Walzer, *Spheres of Justice*, pp. 303–311.

45 See Reinhold Niebuhr, *The Nature and Destiny of Man*, 2 vols. (New York: Charles Scribner's Sons, 1941–1943), ii: *Human Destiny*,

pp. 247–256. For Niebuhr, equality and liberty are transcendent, or regulative, principles of justice.

46 Walzer, *Spheres of Justice*, p. 321.
47 Reinhold Niebuhr, *The Children of Light and the Children of Darkness* (New York: Scribner's, 1960), p. xiii.
48 Wood, *Creation of the American Republic*, pp. 120–121; cf. pp. 426–429.
49 Compare Heinz-Horst Schrey, Hans Herman Walz, and W. A. Whitehouse, *The Biblical Doctrine of Justice and Law* (London: S. C. M. Press, 1955), pp. 182–183.

Select bibliography

Allen, Joseph L., *Love and Conflict: A Covenantal Model of Christian Ethics*, Nashville: Abingdon Press, 1984.

Ames, William, *Conscience with the Power and Cases Thereof. Divided into V Books*. Translated out of Latin into English, 1639.

Andolsen, Barbara Hilbert, Christine E. Gudorf, and Mary D. Pellauer (eds.), *Women's Consciousness, Women's Conscience: A Reader in Feminist Ethics*, San Francisco: Harper & Row, 1985.

Aquinas, Thomas, *Summa Theologiae*, vol. XXXVII: *Justice* (2a2ae. 57–62), ed. Thomas Gilby, O.P., Cambridge: Blackfriars, 1975.

Aristotle, *Politics*, New York: Random House, The Modern Library edn., 1943.

The Nicomachean Ethics, trans. J. E. C. Weldon, Buffalo, New York: Prometheus Books, 1987.

Ashcraft, Richard, *Revolutionary Politics and Locke's Two Treatises of Government*, Princeton University Press, 1986.

(ed.), *John Locke: Critical Assessments*, 4 vols., London: Routledge, 1991.

Bailyn, Bernard, *The Ideological Origins of the American Revolution*, Cambridge, Massachusetts: Harvard University Press, 1967.

Ball, Milner, *The Promise of American Law: A Theological, Humanistic View of Legal Process*, Athens, Georgia: The University of Georgia Press, 1981.

Baxter, Richard, *A Holy Commonwealth*, London, 1659.

How to do Good to Many, or The Public Good is the Christian Life. Directions and Motives to it, London, 1682.

Bell, Derrick, *And We Are Not Saved: The Elusive Quest for Racial Justice*, New York: Basic Books, 1989.

Faces at the Bottom of the Well: The Permanence of Racism, New York: Basic Books, 1992.

Bellah, Robert N., *The Broken Covenant: American Civil Religion in Time of Trial*, New York: Seabury, 1975.

Bellah, Robert N., Richard Madsen, William M. Sullivan, Ann Swidler, and Steven M. Tipton, *The Good Society*, New York: Alfred Knopf, 1991.

Habits of the Heart: Individualism and Commitment in American Life, Berkeley: University of California Press, 1985.

Berman, Harold J., *Faith and Order: The Reconciliation of Law and Religion*, Atlanta, Georgia: Scholars Press, 1993.

Law and Revolution: The Formation of the Western Legal Tradition, Cambridge, Massachusetts: Harvard University Press, 1983.

Breen, T. H., *The Character of the Good Ruler: A Study of Puritan Political Ideas in New England, 1630–1730*, New Haven: Yale University Press, 1970.

Breward, Ian (ed.), *The Works of William Perkins*, Appleford, Abingdon: The Sutton Courtenay Press, 1970.

Cahill, Lisa Sowle, *Between the Sexes: Foundations for a Christian Ethics of Sexuality*, Philadelphia: Fortress Press, 1985.

Calvin, John, *Calvin's Commentaries on The Epistles of Paul the Apostle to the Romans and to the Thessalonians*, trans. Ross Mackenzie and ed. David W. Torrance and Thomas F. Torrance, Edinburgh: Oliver & Boyd, 1960.

Institutes of the Christian Religion, seventh American edn., 2 vols., Philadelphia: Presbyterian Board of Christian Education, 1936.

Carter, Stephen L., *The Culture of Disbelief: How American Law and Politics Trivialize Religious Devotion*, New York: Basic Books, 1993.

Childs, Brevard S., *The Book of Exodus: A Critical Theological Commentary*, Philadelphia: The Westminster Press, 1974.

Clements, R. E., *Prophecy and Tradition*, Atlanta, Georgia: John Knox Press, 1975.

Colman, John, *John Locke's Moral Philosophy*, Edinburgh University Press, 1983.

Cone, James H., *Black Theology and Black Power*, New York: The Seabury Press, 1969.

Martin & Malcolm & America: A Dream or a Nightmare? Maryknoll, New York: Orbis Books, 1993.

Cronin, Kieran, *Rights and Christian Ethics*, Cambridge University Press, 1992.

Curran, Charles E., and Richard A. McCormick, S. J., (eds.), *Natural Law and Theology* (*Readings in Moral Theology*, No. 7), New York: Paulist Press, 1991.

Dahl, Robert A., *Democracy and Its Critics*, New Haven: Yale University Press, 1989.

Daley, Lois K. (ed.), *Feminist Theological Ethics: A Reader*, Louisville, Kentucky: Westminster John Knox Press, 1994.

Davidow, Robert P. (ed.), *Natural Rights and Natural Law: The Legacy of George Mason*, Fairfax, Virginia: George Mason University Press, 1986.

172   *Select bibliography*

Del Vecchio, Georgio, *Justice: An Historical and Philosophical Essay*, Edinburgh University Press, 1952.
Douglass, R. Bruce, Gerald M. Mara, and Henry Richardson (eds.), *Liberalism and the Good*, New York: Routledge, 1990.
Dunn, John, "Justice and the Interpretation of Locke's Political Theory," *Political Studies* 16:1 (1968), pp. 68–87.
The Political Thought of John Locke, Cambridge University Press, 1969.
Dworkin, Ronald, *Taking Human Rights Seriously*, Cambridge, Massachusetts: Harvard University Press, 1977.
Eichrodt, Walther, *Theology of the Old Testament*, 2 vols., Philadelphia: The Westminster Press, 1961.
Emerson, Everett H., "Calvin and Covenant," *Church History* 25 (1956), pp. 136–144.
Everett, William Johnson, *God's Federal Republic: Reconstructing Our Governing Symbol*, New York: Paulist Press, 1988.
Farley, Margaret A., *Personal Commitments: Beginning, Keeping, Changing*, San Francisco: Harper & Row, 1986.
Farmer, James, *Lay Bare the Heart: An Autobiography of the Civil Rights Movement*, New York: Arbor House, 1985.
Fiorenza, Elizabeth Schüssler, *In Memory of Her: A Feminist Theological Reconstruction of Christian Origins*, New York: Crossroad, 1983.
Firmage, Edwin Brown, Bernard G. Weiss, and John W. Welch (eds.), *Religion and Law: Biblical-Judaic and Islamic Perspectives*, Winona Lake: Eisenbrauns, 1990.
Franklin, Robert Michael, *Liberating Visions: Human Fulfilment and Social Justice in African-American Thought*, Minneapolis: Fortress Press, 1990.
Friedrich, Carl, and John W. Chapman (eds.), *Nomos IV. Justice*, New York: Atherton Press, 1963.
Gewirth, Alan, *Human Rights: Essays on Justification and Applications*, The University of Chicago Press, 1982.
Gilligan, Carol, *In a Different Voice: Psychological Theory and Women's Development*, Cambridge, Massachusetts: Harvard University Press, 1982.
Gough, J. W., *John Locke's Political Philosophy*, Oxford University Press, 1973.
Gremillion, Josef (ed.), *The Gospel of Peace and Justice: Catholic Social Teaching Since Pope John*, Maryknoll, New York: Orbis Books, 1976.
Grotius, Hugo, *De jure belli ac pacis*, Paris, 1625.
Gustafson, James M., *Can Ethics Be Christian?*, The University of Chicago Press, 1975.
Ethics from a Theocentric Perspective, 2 vols., The University of Chicago Press, 1981–1984.

Protestant and Roman Catholic Ethics: Prospects for Rapprochement. The University of Chicago Press, 1978.

Harrelson, Walter, *The Ten Commandments and Human Rights*, Philadelphia: Fortress Press, 1980.

Hauerwas, Stanley, *A Community of Character*, Notre Dame, Indiana; University of Notre Dame Press, 1981.

After Christendom? How the Church is to Behave if Freedom, Justice and a Christian Nation Are Bad Ideas, Nashville, Tennessee: Abingdon Press, 1991.

The Peaceable Kingdom, Notre Dame, Indiana: University of Notre Dame Press, 1983.

Heyward, Carter, *Our Passion for Justice: Images of Power, Sexuality, and Liberation*, New York: The Pilgrim Press, 1984.

Hobbes, Thomas, *Leviathan; or The Matter, Form, and Power of a Commonwealth Ecclesiastical and Civil*, in Edwin A. Burtt (ed.), *The English Philosophers from Bacon to Mill*, New York: The Modern Library, 1939.

Holleman, Warren Lee, *The Human Rights Movement: Western Values and Theological Perspectives*, New York: Praeger, 1987.

Hollenbach, David, "The Common Good Revisited," *Theological Studies* 50 (1989), pp. 70–94.

Justice, Peace, and Human Rights: American Catholic Ethics in a Pluralistic World, New York: Crossroad, 1988.

Kelsay, John, and Sumner B. Twiss (eds.), *Religion and Human Rights*, New York: The Project on Religion and Human Rights, 1994.

King, Martin Luther, Jr., *Stride Toward Freedom: The Montgomery Story*, New York: Harper, 1958.

Where Do We Go from Here: Chaos or Community? Boston: Beacon Press, 1968.

Konner, Melvin, *Dear America, A Concerned Doctor Wants You to Know the Truth About Health Reform*, Reading, Massachusetts: Addison-Wesley Publishing Company, 1993.

Lebacqz, Karen, *Six Theories of Justice: Perspectives from Philosophical and Theological Ethics*, Minneapolis: Augsburg Publishing House, 1986.

Levenson, Jon D., *Sinai and Zion: An Entry Into the Jewish Bible*, Minneapolis, Minnesota: Winston Press, 1985.

Levy, Leonard W., and Dennis J. Mahoney (eds.), *The Framing and Ratification of the Constitution*, New York: Macmillan Publishing Company, 1987.

Little, David, *Religion, Order and Law: A Study in Pre-Revolutionary England*, New York: Harper & Row, 1969.

Locke, John, *The Reasonableness of Christianity, as Delivered in the Scriptures*, in

The Works of John Locke, in Nine Volumes, 12th edn. (London, 1824), VI, pp. 1–158.

Two Treatises of Government, ed. Peter Laslett, Cambridge University Press, 2nd edn., 1967.

Lutz, Donald, S., *The Origins of American Constitutionalism*, Baton Rouge,: Louisiana State University Press, 1988.

MacIntyre, Alasdair, *After Virtue: A Study in Moral Theology*, Notre Dame, Indiana: University of Notre Dame Press, 1981.

Whose Justice? Which Rationality?, Notre Dame, Indiana: University of Notre Dame Press, 1988.

McGiffert, Michael, "Covenant, Crown, and Commons in Elizabethan Puritanism," *The Journal of British Studies* 20:1 (Fall, 1980), pp. 32–52.

"Grace and Works: The Rise and Division of Covenant Divinity in Elizabethan Puritanism," *Harvard Theological Review* 75:4 (October, 1982), pp. 463–502.

Malcolm X, *The Autobiography of Malcolm X*, with the assistance of Alex Haley, New York: Ballantine Books, 1964.

Martin, J. Paul (ed.), *Twenty-Five Human Rights Documents*, New York: Columbia University Press, 1994.

Merrill, Thomas F. (ed.), *William Perkins, 1558–1602: English Puritanist. His Pioneer Works on Casuistry: "A Discourse of Conscience" and "The Whole Treatise of Cases of Conscience,"* Nieuwkoop, Netherlands: B. De Graff, 1966.

Miller, Patrick, D., Jr., Paul D. Hanson, and S. Dean McBride (eds.), *Ancient Israelite Religion*, Philadelphia: Fortress Press, 1987.

Miller, Perry (ed.), *The American Puritans: Their Prose and Poetry*, Garden City: Doubleday & Company, Inc., Anchor Books, 1956.

The New England Mind: From Colony to Province, Cambridge, Massachusetts: Harvard University Press, 1953.

The New England Mind: The Seventeenth Century, New York: Macmillan Company, 1939.

Mooney, Christopher F., *Public Virtue: Law and the Social Character of Religion*, Notre Dame, Indiana: University of Notre Dame Press, 1986.

Morgan, Edmund S., *Roger Williams: The Church and the State*, New York: Harcourt, Brace & World, Inc., 1967.

(ed.), *Puritan Political Ideas, 1558–1794*, Indianapolis: The Bobbs-Merrill Company, Inc., 1965.

Nicholson, Ernest W., *God and His People: Covenant and Theology in the Old Testament*, Oxford: Clarendon Press, 1986.

Nickel, James, W., *Making Sense of Human Rights: Philosophical Reflections on the Universal Declaration of Human Rights*, Berkeley: University of California Press, 1987.

Niebuhr, H. Richard, *The Kingdom of God in America*, New York: Harper & Brothers, 1937.
Radical Monotheism and Western Culture with Supplementary Essays, New York: Harper & Brothers, 1960.
The Responsible Self, New York: Harper & Row, 1963.
Niebuhr, Reinhold, *The Nature and Destiny of Man*, 2 vols., New York: Charles Scribner's Sons, 1941–1943.
Okin, Susan Moller, *Justice, Gender, and the Family*, New York: Basic Books, 1989.
Outka, Gene, and John P. Reeder, Jr., (eds.), *Prospects for a Common Morality*, Princeton University Press, 1993.
Pegis, Anton C. (ed.), *The Basic Writings of Saint Thomas Aquinas*, 2 vols., New York: Random House, 1945.
Perelman, C., *The Idea of Justice and the Problem of Argument*, London: Routledge & Paul, 1963.
Perry, Michael J., *Love and Power: The Role of Religion and Morality in American Politics*, New York: Oxford University Press, 1991.
Pettit, Norman, *The Heart Prepared: Grace and Conversion in Puritan Spiritual Life*, New Haven: Yale University Press, 1966.
Pieper, Josef, *The Four Cardinal Virtues*, Notre Dame, Indiana: University of Notre Dame Press, 1966.
Pocock, J. G. A., *The Machiavellian Moment: Florentine Political Thought and the Atlantic Republican Tradition*, Princeton University Press, 1975.
Popper, Stephen, *World Hypotheses*, Berkeley: University of California Press, 1961.
Preston, John, *The New Covenant, or The Saints' Portion. A Treatise Concerning the All Sufficiency of God, Man's Righteousness, and the Covenant of Grace*, The Eighth Edition corrected, London, 1634.
Sermons Preached Before His Majestie, and upon other speciall occasions, London, 1634.
Ramsey, Paul, *Basic Christian Ethics*, New York: Charles Scribner's Sons, 1950.
Rawls, John, *A Theory of Justice*, Cambridge, Massachusetts: Harvard University Press, 1971.
Richter, Melvin, *The Political Thought of Montesquieu*, Cambridge University Press, 1977.
Rorty, Richard, J. B. Schneewind, and Quentin Skinner (eds.), *Philosophy and History*, Cambridge University Press, 1984.
Russell, Letty M., *Human Liberation in a Feminist Perspective – A Theology*, Philadelphia: The Westminster Press, 1974.
Schechter, Stephen L. (ed.), *Roots of the Republic: American Founding Documents Interpreted*, contributing editors: Richard B. Bernstein and Donald S. Lutz, Madison, Wisconsin: Madison House, 1990.

Schrey, Heinz-Horst, Hans Herman Walz, and W. A. Whitehouse, *The Biblical Doctrine of Justice and Law*, London: S. C. M. Press, 1955.

Sibbes, Richard, *Works of Richard Sibbes*, edited with memoir by Alexander B. Grosart, 7 vols., Edinburgh, 1862–1864.

Stoever, William K. B., *"A Faire and Easie Way to Heaven": Covenant Theology and Antinomianism in Massachusetts*, Middleton, Connecticut: Wesleyan University Press, 1978.

Stokes, Anson Phelps, *Church and State in the United States*, 3 vols., New York: Harper & Brothers, 1950.

Strauss, Leo, *Natural Right and History*, University of Chicago Press, 1953.

Tocqueville, Alexis de, *Democracy in America*, 2 vols., London, 1838.

Trinterud, Leonard J., "The Origins of Puritanism," *Church History* 20:1 (March, 1951), pp. 37–57.

Tully, James, *A Discourse on Property: John Locke and His Adversaries*, Cambridge University Press, 1980.

Villa-Vicencio, Charles, *A Theology of Reconstruction: Nation-Building and Human Rights*, Cambridge University Press, 1992.

von Leyden, W. (ed.), *John Locke: Essays on the Law of Nature*, Oxford: Clarendon Press, 1954.

von Rad, Gerhard, *Old Testament Theology*, 2 vols., New York: Harper & Brothers, 1962–1965.

Walzer, Michael, *Exodus and Revolution*, New York: Basic Books, Inc., 1985.

The Revolution of the Saints: A Study in the Origins of Radical Politics, Cambridge, Massachusetts: Harvard University Press, 1965.

Spheres of Justice: A Defense of Pluralism and Equality, New York: Basic Books, 1983.

West, Cornel, *Prophesy Deliverance! An Afro-American Revolutionary Christianity*, Philadelphia: The Westminster Press, 1982.

Wise, John, *A Vindication of the Government of the New England Churches, and the Churches' Quarrel Espoused; or, a Reply to Certain Proposals*, Boston: Congregational Board of Publications, 1860.

Wood, Gordon, S., *The Creation of the American Republic 1776–1787*, Chapel Hill: The University of North Carolina Press, 1969.

Woodhouse, A. S. P. (ed.), *Puritanism and Liberty, Being the Army Debates (1647–9) from the Clarke Manuscripts with Supplementary Documents*, The University of Chicago Press, 1951.

Zaret, David, *The Heavenly Contract: Ideology and Organization in Pre-Revolutionary Puritanism*, The University of Chicago Press, 1985.

Index